DM

DELANCEY

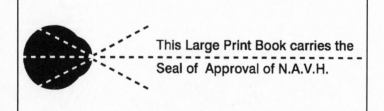

This Large Print Book carries the
Seal of Approval of N.A.V.H.

DELANCEY

A MAN, A WOMAN,
A RESTAURANT, A MARRIAGE

MOLLY WIZENBERG

THORNDIKE PRESS

A part of Gale, Cengage Learning

GALE
CENGAGE Learning®

Farmington Hills, Mich • San Francisco • New York • Waterville, Maine
Meriden, Conn • Mason, Ohio • Chicago

GALE
CENGAGE Learning®

LIBRARY OF CONGRESS CATALOGING-IN-PUBLICATION DATA

Wizenberg, Molly.
    Delancey : a man, a woman, a restaurant, a marriage / by Molly Wizenberg.
        pages cm (Thorndike press large print biography)
    ISBN 978-1-4104-7204-5 (hardcover) — ISBN 1-4104-7204-3 (hardcover)
    1. Delancey (Pizzeria : Seattle, Wash.) 2. Pizzerias—Washington (State)—Seattle. 3. Wizenberg, Molly. 4. Pettit, Brandon. 5. Restaurateurs—United States—Biography. 6. Food writers—United States—Biography. 7. Large type books. I. Title.
    TX945.5.D38W59 2014b
    647.95092—dc23
    [B]   2014016061

Published in 2014 by arrangement with Simon & Schuster, Inc.

Printed in the United States of America
1 2 3 4 5 6 7 18 17 16 15 14

For Brandon

It may be that when we no longer know what to do, we have come to our real work, and when we no longer know which way to go, we have begun our real journey. The mind that is not baffled is not employed. The impeded stream is the one that sings.

— WENDELL BERRY

A NOTE ABOUT THE RECIPES IN THIS BOOK

You are holding a book about the birth of a restaurant, and my guess is that you're probably expecting to see some recipes from that restaurant. There will be a few, but here's the truth: when you're opening a restaurant, you might be surrounded by food, but you don't often get to eat it. You're too busy, or it's too expensive and you're saving it for your customers. During the period of our lives that you'll read about here, Brandon and I ate a lot of beans and rice at a taqueria in our neighborhood, and a lot of Vietnamese and Thai takeout. Even after Delancey was up and running, our diet consisted largely of scraps and leftovers, or the pizzas that weren't good enough to serve to paying customers. (At the restaurant, we have a name for those pizzas: "love pies," because the only person they're fit for is someone who already loves you and doesn't mind that dinner looks like a volcanic eruption.)

A few of the recipes in this book are for dishes that we served at Delancey early on, when I cooked there. But in large part, what you'll find here are the foods that we *wished* we were eating. You'll also find dishes that friends made for us when we were too crazed to cook for ourselves. And you'll find the recipes that we turn to most often now, when we don't have a lot of time to cook together but still want to make the most of the time we do have. All in all, these recipes are about a satisfying kind of economy: the day-to-day economy, time-wise and money-wise, of a real home kitchen. They're about making something great from what you've got: maybe a carton of day-old takeout rice, a doggie bag of barbecued pork, and a bunch of kale from last Sunday's market. The recipes here are straightforward but big-flavored, the way we like to cook. Most of them come together quickly, and even those that take longer require little tending.

One more thing: a note about salt. At Delancey, we use Diamond Crystal brand kosher salt in almost everything, and I use it frequently at home, too, because it's cheap, easy to pinch between your fingers, and comes in seemingly bottomless boxes.

But different brands of kosher salt have very different crystal sizes, and that can make kosher salt tricky to quantify in recipes. So, for the sake of simplicity, I have written the recipes in this book to use fine-grained salt — either fine sea salt or table salt. My preference is for the former, and I use La Baleine brand, in the blue cardboard canister. I'm not a great fan of table salt, because it doesn't taste very good, but sometimes it's all you've got. A couple of recipes also call for a crunchy finishing salt like Maldon or *fleur de sel,* but that's mostly for the sake of texture. If you don't have any, don't worry about it.

INTRODUCTION

I dug out my wedding vows the other night. I hadn't read them since we got married, and our fifth anniversary is coming up. I wanted to see if I was holding up my end of the deal. Brandon and I each wrote our own vows, agreeing on just a rough word count and leaving the rest a surprise, and we read them to each other for the first time during the ceremony, in front of our assembled families and friends.

Wedding vows were made to be said aloud, and when you look at somebody's vows written out — anybody's, even your own — they tend to read like a Hallmark card. In my vows, I told Brandon that he's the best person I know, and that when I describe him to someone new, the first thing I say is, "He's so *good.*" I told him that I love the fact that he whistles constantly, without knowing that he's doing it. I love that he's been singing the same Caetano

Veloso song in the shower since we met, and that he still can't get the lyrics right. I love that he's the first person our friends call when they're in trouble. I love that he likes to make people happy. My mother once told me that the reason she fell in love with my father was that she knew she could always learn from him. When I met Brandon, I knew what she meant.

Explaining why I love Brandon was easy. But then came the tricky part of the vows, the part where I had to make the kind of promises that make you married. I remember the day that I wrote that part, because it made me very nervous. Not that that's a real problem: I've always thought marriage was a fine thing to be nervous about. There's nothing breezy about "until death do us part." You're hitching your wagon to someone else's, and if you're totally honest about it, neither of you really knows how the steering column works, which road you'd be smartest to take, and whether, somewhere down that road, your spouse's wheel hubs will open to reveal blades designed specifically to tear your wagon apart, *Ben Hur*-style. I see trepidation as a mark of sanity. But that's why I forged ahead and wrote what I did: because I knew all of that, and still I wanted to get married. So I told him that I would always love him and support him, even though the word *always* makes me feel like I need an antacid. I wanted to say it. I wanted to believe it. I vowed to work with him to make our hopes and dreams real, whatever they might be, and I meant it.

I had already had a preview of Brandon's hopes and dreams. When we met in the spring of 2005, he was twenty-three and living in New York, and I was twenty-six and living in Seattle. He was a trained saxophonist and composer, working on a master's degree in composition. I worked in publishing, wrote a food blog, and was slowly extracting myself from a doctoral program that I'd decided not to finish. We both loved to cook and eat. Brandon was particularly into espresso. He had three espresso machines and a commercial-grade grinder that was larger than some New York kitchens, each one carefully researched and purchased on eBay. The first time I took him to visit my mother, he spent an entire afternoon working on my dad's old Faema Contessa, which hadn't been touched in the three years since he died. A bolt in the housing was stuck, and Brandon wrestled with it for most of an afternoon. When it came loose, he made my mother a cappuccino, and then he grinned for a week.

But about a year after we met, when we moved in together in Seattle, he started noticing that caffeine made him feel like the Hulk, like yelling and smashing things and wearing tight purple pants. So he gave up espresso and sold his fancy machines. Instead, he decided, he would build violins. He'd always loved the instrument: the romance of it, the sound of it, the fact that it's notoriously difficult to build well. Brandon loves a good problem. He was starting a PhD program in composition at the University of Washington that fall, and he had a job at a restaurant, but building violins, he thought, would be a nice way to spend his free time.

After we settled into our first apartment, he built a work-bench from plywood and two-by-fours in the basement. He bought chisels and planes of every size. Whenever we were out in the car, he pulled over at every garage sale, shopping for tools. He bought books on violins. He bought a broken violin and broke it even more, studying the way the parts fit together. On Craigslist, he found an ad for a specialized drill, eighteen inches long and closely resembling a milkshake blender, and one afternoon, we met up with the guy who was

16

selling it, handed him a few twenties, and heaved it out of the back of his truck.

But Brandon didn't build a violin, or a fraction of a violin. Once he understood *how* to build one, once he'd gone through the steps in his head, once he'd solved the problem, he was satisfied. The tools lay dormant through the winter, and then, when summer came around again, Brandon announced a new idea: he was going to build a boat.

Since moving to Seattle, he'd bought himself a membership to the Center for Wooden Boats, and anytime he had a few hours free, he'd rent a boat and go out rowing on Lake Union. He wanted to have his own boat someday, and given that such things are not cheap, the best bet, he decided, was to build one. Our friend Sam would help, and they would do it in the backyard of our apartment, using plans for a traditional Australian skiff that Brandon bought online. This was 2007, the summer of our wedding, and it was going to be a busy summer. But as he pointed out, the boat would be fun for both of us: it would be a mobile picnic table! (He knows what I like.) Plus, he wouldn't even have to buy tools! He could use the stuff he'd bought for the violins! It was perfect! I had no reason to argue. I looked forward to the picnics.

I also looked forward to the ice cream shop that he was going to open. He'd been into making ice cream since I met him — since before then, actually, when he spent a few months studying in Paris and lived in an apartment down the street from the famous Berthillon ice cream shop. The first year that we were dating, he bought me an Italian gelato maker for my birthday — one of those buy-your-partner-the-gift-that-you-yourself-would-like-to-receive scenarios, though I didn't mind — and on his next visit, he christened it with a batch of bourbon-spiked pear sorbet. By the time he moved to Seattle, he was well on his way to perfecting his favorite ice cream flavor, salted caramel. He'd noticed that Seattle didn't have a great local ice cream company, like Berthillon or San Francisco's Bi-Rite Creamery, and he began to think, *Hey, I could do something about that.* So when he wasn't reading up on boat design, he researched local health code regulations, methods, and industrial-grade machines.

But he didn't build the boat or open the ice cream shop. Brandon and I got married, and then we went on a honeymoon to Vancouver Island, and then summer was over. I

18

had left my publishing job and was writing my first book, a memoir about growing up in a food-loving family and losing my dad. Brandon was in his second year of the PhD program, working as a teaching assistant, leading music classes two days a week at a Montessori elementary school, teaching on Saturday mornings at a conservatory program for teenagers, and still working at a local restaurant. We were happy, working hard, learning how to be adults, figuring out what it meant to be married. Things were humming along. And then one night that fall, over a late dinner at our friend Carla's restaurant that ended with us dancing to Blondie in the darkened, empty dining room, Brandon and Carla hatched the idea of opening a pizza place.

A pizza place? What we had here was a giant violin! Or maybe, *maybe,* a picnic boat offering ice cream by the scoop.

A little over a year later, Sam took a picture of us. Brandon is on a ladder in what is now the kitchen of Delancey, tiling the face of the wood-burning pizza oven. I'm standing below him, holding a power drill. He looks tired, a little worried, possibly in mid-sentence. I'm staring at something outside the frame, absolutely expressionless. But I know what I was thinking: *Holy shit.*

19

1

If you want to get Brandon's family talking, you need only ask about his childhood tantrums, *aaannnnnnnd they're off!* Their descriptions are sufficiently vivid that you'd think he'd had a screaming meltdown in the family car last week. But if you ask Brandon about his tantrums, he'll tell you that he was constantly hungry, and that low blood sugar will bring out the wailing, shrieking lunatic in anyone. When he was eight or nine, he taught himself to cope by cooking. And his parents, who weren't especially interested in cooking, rewarded his initiative, because in the Pettit household of Upper Saddle River, New Jersey, whoever cooked dinner didn't have to do the cleanup afterward.

Anyway, while most of his peers were off wrestling in the yard, breaking things, or lighting household pets on fire, Brandon got a lot of positive attention for cooking. His uncle Tom offered to teach him how to make a few dishes, and so did his mother's friend Ellen. His best friend Steve's mother, Laura, taught him how to make *penne alla vodka* when he was in middle school. Afterward, before he went home, she dumped out a small Poland Spring water bottle, refilled it with vodka, and gave it to him so that he could make the recipe for his parents. His mother found it in his backpack later that night, and you know how that story goes.

Meanwhile, I grew up 1,500 miles to the west, in Oklahoma City, Oklahoma, the only child in a family so preoccupied with cooking and eating that we would regularly spend dinner discussing what we might eat the following night. My parents met in Baltimore and courted over oysters and pan-fried shad roe, and though they had lived in the land of waving wheat and chicken-fried steak since a few years before I was born, they took pleasure in introducing me to lobster, croissants, and Dover sole. My father was a radiation oncologist, and he worked full-time until he was nearly seventy, but most evenings, after pouring himself a Scotch and thumbing absentmindedly through the mail, he made dinner. It wasn't necessarily fancy — there were hamburgers and salad and cans of baked beans, and his macaroni and cheese involved a brick of Velveeta — but the kitchen was where he went to relax, to unwind from a day of seeing patients. He was a good cook. My mother is also a good cook, a very good cook, but I think of her mostly as a baker. She made brownies and crisps and birthday cakes, and in our neighborhood she became something of a legend for the elaborate cookies and candies she made each Christmas. Food was how the three of us spent time together. Cooking and eating gave our days their rhythm and consistency, and the kitchen was where everything happened. As a baby, I played on the floor with pots and spoons while my mother cooked. The three of us sat down to dinner at the kitchen table nearly every night (except Thursdays, when my parents went out and left me with a Stouffer's Turkey Tetrazzini and Julia Beal, the elderly babysitter, who always arrived with a floral-patterned plastic bonnet tied under her chin), and we kept up the habit (minus Stouffer's and Mrs. Beal, after a certain point) until I went to college.

I started cooking with my parents when I was in high school. I was not what you would call a difficult teen: Friday night might find me baking a cake or holed up in my bedroom with my notebook of poems. If I felt like doing something really exciting, I might invite some friends over and make a rhubarb cobbler. When I was seventeen, Food Network came into existence, and then I spent hour after hour watching cooking shows, which fueled even more baking and a poem about immersing myself in a vat of Marshmallow Fluff.

Brandon's teenage years were a little more interesting — he regularly handed in his homework late — but he too watched a lot of cooking shows. This was back in the golden age when you could actually learn something from Food Network — when David Rosengarten's brilliant *Taste* was still on the air and Emeril Lagasse's show was taped on a modest set without a studio audience, live musicians, or abuse of the word *bam*. Brandon learned about extra virgin olive oil on *Molto Mario* and balsamic vinegar on *Essence of Emeril* and begged his parents to add them to the grocery list. He once watched a show about soups during which the host reeled off a number of tricks for adding flavor and body: add a Parmigiano-Reggiano rind or a *bouquet garni,* for example, or drop in a potato, toss in some dried mushrooms, or simmer a teabag in the stock. Armed with this information, he decided to combine all of the tricks in a single soup, surely the greatest soup the world would ever know. The result, he reports, was very flavorful, like run-off from a large-scale mining operation.

Growing up, Brandon had four favorite pizza places: Posa Posa, Martio's, and Michaelangelo's, all in Nanuet, New York; and Kinchley's, in Ramsey, New Jersey. Of course, every kid on earth loves pizza, and a lot of them probably have four favorite pizza joints. But I know of few eight-year-olds who want to interview the *pizzaiolo*. Brandon took dance classes as a kid, and the ballet studio was conveniently located a few doors down from Michaelangelo's. After class, he would pummel the owner with questions. *What's in the dough? What do you put in the sauce? Why do you grate the mozzarella for the cheese pizza, instead of slicing it?* In exchange for answers and free slices, he agreed to put coupons under the windshield wipers of cars in the parking lot out front.

But if it were all really that straightforward, if Brandon and I had both homed in on food from the get-go, and if he had known that he would be a chef and I had known that I would someday own a restaurant with my chef husband, this would be a

25

boring story, and I would not be telling it.

Maybe even more than he loved to cook, Brandon loved to dance. His mother, wanting to expose her son to a little bit of everything, started him in dance classes as a very young kid, and by the time he was a preteen, he was on track to someday join a touring company. Down the line, he'd decided, he would be a choreographer. Choreography and cooking pushed the same buttons in him: they were both about *making things,* about taking a series of separate elements and assembling them in a particular sequence to make something appealing and new. As a middle schooler, he took upwards of eight hours of dance classes a week, and sometimes, depending on the season, he took as many as twenty. When he was twelve, he got into a prestigious summer program at the Pennsylvania Ballet school. Each afternoon, when he was supposed to be resting, he sneaked into the classes for older teens, where he got to partner with female dancers. This was the big time. One day, while doing some sort of move that you're not supposed to do when you're twelve, he fractured one of the vertebrae in his lower back. The upshot was that he couldn't dance for the better part of a year, and as further punishment, he had to wear a plastic torso brace that made him look like Tom Hanks's deranged secretary in *Splash,* the one who wore her bra over her clothes.

He couldn't do anything that required much mobility, but he could still cook. He could also practice the saxophone. In addition to dance, he'd taken music lessons — piano and saxophone — since he was a kid. Now, while sidelined from ballet, he began to practice for hours a day. After school, he'd go down to the basement, put on Pink Floyd's "Money," and play along, over and over, with the sax solo that starts at 2:04. Or he'd go to Tower Records and fish around in the discount bin for classic R&B and blues CDs, Charlie Parker or T-Bone Walker, and then he'd play along to those too. He sometimes went to the ballet studio to watch a class, to try to keep his head in it, but he began to notice that, maybe more than the physical movement itself, what he liked about dance was the music. Music was underneath all of it.

By the time he started thinking about college, he was spending most of his non-school hours playing the saxophone, and when he wasn't playing the saxophone, he was cooking. He thought about going to culinary school instead of college, but he'd been a vegetarian since birth — his parents, siblings, and most of his extended family are vegetarian — and while he didn't want to cook meat, he also wasn't interested in seeking out a specialized vegetarian culinary school, which seemed limiting in the long run. Anyway, he would always cook, he reasoned, whether or not he was a trained chef. He would always need to eat. But if he wanted to keep at his music, and if he wanted to go somewhere with it, he would need formal training. So he decided to try for a conservatory slot in saxophone, upping his practice schedule from a couple of hours a day to three or four. There's a video taken around that time, at his high school's Battle of the Bands. I wish you could see it. Brandon is seventeen, singing lead and straddling the sax in a band called "Ummm . . . ," and he's deep in his Jim Morrison phase, with dark sunglasses, long curly brown hair, and his shirt unbuttoned to the navel, for which he would later get detention.

The following year, he moved to Ohio as a freshman at Oberlin College Conservatory of Music. He declared a major in saxophone performance, but the urge to *make* something — not just memorize and perform a piece of music that someone else had made — was still there, and in his second year, he added a minor in music composition. After graduation, he moved to New York to work on a master's at Brooklyn College Conservatory, sharing an apartment in Manhattan with a violinist and an opera singer. Meanwhile, I had left Oklahoma City and headed west to Stanford, where I studied human biology and French and was frequently asleep in my dorm room bunk bed by ten o'clock, though I did flirt with rebellion by cutting my hair short, dyeing it calico, and stealing pre-portioned balls of Otis Spunkmeyer cookie dough from the freezer of my dining hall. When I graduated, I spent a year teaching English in France before moving to Seattle in 2002 to start graduate school in anthropology at the University of Washington.

Brandon and I met in 2005, when a friend of his suggested that he read *Orangette,* the food blog that I had started the previous summer. He did, and then he sent an e-mail to pass on a few choice compliments that evidently were very effective. He described himself as "a musician (composer) getting my master's part-time in NYC, while being a full-time food snob / philosopher / chef." Let's ignore the snob / philosopher part; he was only twenty-three, so he gets a pass.

But the chef part! He was referring, I would learn, to his part-time job as a cooking-and-grocery-shopping go-fer for a wealthy uncle, and to the fact that he liked to have friends over to dinner. But, people: *I should have seen it.* This man was not going to be a composer. By the second letter, he was describing the smell of flaming Calvados on crêpes, and to explain what type of music he wrote, he offered this:

I guess it's considered classical. I usually write for choirs or orchestras or chamber groups, although sometimes I use electronics or make sound sculptures or installations. For a food analogy: I won't make salads with raw chicken, lychee, pork rinds, and lemon zest with a motor oil, goat cheese, and olive oil dressing, just because no one has done it before. I try to make "dishes" that taste like nothing else, and taste good. Being a composer is really no different from being a chef or a choreographer.

I should have seen it, but I didn't. And until a few months after we were married, I don't think he did, either.

PENNE ALLA VODKA

I am sorry to report that Brandon no longer remembers the recipe he was taught as a teenager. But once, on a trip to Florida for his cousin's wedding, we ate a first-rate *penne alla vodka* at an Italian restaurant called Tramonti, and this recipe is based on our memory of that one. For everyday purposes, we like to make the sauce with half a cup of cream, which yields a creamy-tasting result without veering into special-occasion territory. In a restaurant, they'd probably use more, and you're welcome to experiment.

If you have a box grater, pull it out for this recipe. The cheese should be grated very fine, almost to a powder, and the rasp side of a box grater is the best way to do it.

One 28-ounce can whole peeled San Marzano tomatoes, strained, juices discarded
2 medium cloves garlic, pressed
1/2 teaspoon sugar, or to taste
1/4 teaspoon fine sea salt, plus more for cooking the pasta and finishing the sauce
1/2 teaspoon red wine vinegar, or to taste
Pinch of dried oregano
3 tablespoons (42 g) unsalted butter
2 ounces (55 g) pancetta, chopped
Half a medium yellow onion (about 125 g),

finely chopped
Pinch of red pepper flakes
1/2 cup (120 ml) vodka
1/2 cup (120 ml) heavy cream
2 grinds of black pepper
1/4 cup (14 g) packed fresh basil leaves,
   roughly chopped
12 ounces (340 g) penne rigate
2/3 cup (55 g) finely grated Parmigiano-
   Reggiano or Grana Padano

In the bowl of a food processor, combine the tomatoes, garlic, sugar, salt, vinegar, and dried oregano. Blend until smooth. Taste: If it's slightly sour or bitter, add a bit more sugar. If it tastes flat, add a bit more vinegar.

Set a large pot of salted water on high heat. (It should taste pleasantly salted, a little less salty than seawater.)

Warm a Dutch oven (or other wide pan with a capacity of about 5 quarts) over medium heat. Add the butter, and when it has melted and is beginning to foam, add the pancetta. Cook, stirring, until the pancetta begins to crisp, about 5 minutes. Add the onion and the red pepper flakes, and cook, stirring occasionally, until the onion is soft and translucent, about 5 minutes. Raise the heat to medium-high, and add the vodka. Cook 3 minutes, stirring regularly.

Add the cream and black pepper, and simmer to thicken slightly, about 2 minutes. Stir in the tomato mixture and the basil, and simmer briskly, stirring occasionally, for 15 minutes.

When the sauce has simmered for a few minutes, put the pasta into the pot of boiling water and cook until al dente, about 12 minutes.

Drain the pasta, and add it to the pot of sauce. Stir in the Parmigiano-Reggiano. Taste for salt, and adjust as needed. Serve immediately.

Yield: 3 to 4 servings

2

For the first fifteen months that Brandon and I were together, we weren't actually together: he was in New York and I was in Seattle. Neither of us had much in the way of extra cash, but we took turns flying to see each other every month or six weeks, over long weekends or holidays. The first time I went to visit him, he took me to Di Fara.

"This pizza," he told me solemnly, "it'll change your life."

I'd known Brandon for less than two months, but I already could have told you that he says this kind of thing on a regular basis. That early summer night, as we rattled through the subway tunnels from Manhattan to Brooklyn, I had no way of knowing that when he said that the pizza at Di Fara would change my life, it would, you know, actually change my life.

I could appreciate his enthusiasm, though

I could only cautiously return it. Pizza is nice, but I had never before considered spending an hour and a half in an overheated New York City subway car just to eat a couple of slices. Where I grew up, the state meal involves fried okra, black-eyed peas, and chicken-fried steak. My childhood pizza education came mostly from Domino's, or from the Tony's brand frozen pizzas with "hamburger"-flavored topping that I was allowed to eat on nights when my parents were out, if I wasn't having turkey tetrazzini.

"You'll see," he assured me. "It's the best thing you'll ever put in your mouth."

Di Fara Pizza is a one-man show, owned and operated since 1965 by Domenico De-Marco, a slightly stooped septuagenarian with flour on his shoes. His kids might take your order or make change or stir a pot in the back kitchen, but he's the only one who touches the pies. We arrived around nine o'clock, and the small, fluorescent-lit shop was still working its way through the evening rush. We took our place in the crowd that stood pressed against the chest-high counter separating DeMarco's giant electric oven from the dingy dining room. (Di Fara is not a fancy place, nor is it a pretty one: its five or six folding tables are generally covered with smears of grease and Parmigiano-

Reggiano dust.) DeMarco was alone behind the counter, shuffling back and forth from the workbench to the oven, tending his pies. The man is deliberate. He does not (and probably, at this point, physically *cannot*) move quickly. No one said a word as we waited, at least two dozen of us, watching him the way a pack of lions watches a grazing zebra.

DeMarco makes pizzas in two styles: traditional New York round, and square (also called Sicilian-style). Brandon ordered us a couple slices of each, despite the fact that there was prosciutto in the sauce for the square pizza.[*] He would not, he whispered, let vegetarianism get between him and a Di Fara pie.

The square pizza at Di Fara is a complex, multi-step thing: a 1/2-inch-thick crust pressed out into a pan, topped with a long-

[*] Vegetarians, take note: DeMarco's daughter Maggie, who helps to run the business, recently told me that because of the number of vegetarians who come to Di Fara, they stopped using prosciutto in the square sauce in 2005 or 2006. I suppose there's a good chance, then, that the slices we ate had no prosciutto? Either way, there's no way to know: the sauce was wonderfully stewy and rich.

simmered San Marzano tomato sauce, slices of fresh mozzarella cut from a fist-sized ball, slices of aged mozzarella, grated Parmigiano-Reggiano or Grana Padano that he feeds through a hand-cranked grater as he goes, plenty of olive oil poured from a copper jug, and fresh herbs snipped with scissors. It's sort of like focaccia — focaccia that oozes so much cheese and tomato that you need a knife, a fork, and three napkins to eat it. By the time we had dispatched our slices, I was prepared to eat anything that Brandon Pettit told me to.

The round pizza was even better. "Viff iss *incredible,*" I said, mid-chew. DeMarco paints the crust with an uncooked tomato sauce, lays slices of aged mozzarella and fresh mozzarella on top, and gives it all a generous splash of olive oil before he slides it into the oven. Minutes later, after he pulls the baked pie from the oven with his bare hands, he sprinkles it with grated Parmigiano-Reggiano or Grana Padano and snips fresh basil on top. The thin crust puffs at the rim, taking on a texture not unlike a good baguette: crisp where it greets the tooth but chewy on the inside, flecked with bubbles. It's Neapolitan-style-meets-New-York-style, bendy but not floppy, mottled with char along the rim and underside. We ate, and then Brandon ducked into a convenience store down the block for a couple of cold beers, and then we thought, *Oh, what the hell,* and ordered two more slices.

It was only later that Brandon explained how much it meant to him that I had liked Di Fara. Shortly before we met, he had taken another girl there on a date, and she wasn't enthused. They broke up shortly afterward. "I felt like she didn't understand me," he confessed. I thought he was exaggerating for emphasis, but as it turns out, Brandon isn't the only one: a New Yorker friend of ours says that she once had the very same response to a date who didn't like Di Fara. It's not a place that people are neutral about. If you do a search online, you'll find page upon page of heated arguments about Di Fara, about whether De-Marco uses Parmigiano-Reggiano or Grana Padano (either, depending on the day), whether he uses buffalo mozzarella or cow's milk mozzarella (sometimes both, and sometimes only the latter), how many cheeses he uses in all (three or four, depending on whether he's got buffalo mozzarella on hand; see previous argument), whether his pizzas are pleasantly charred or burnt to the point of unpleasantness (the former, mostly, though the latter does happen; the guy is *old*), whether his pizzas are overrated or God's own personal gift to the borough of Brooklyn (*make it stop make it stop make it stop*).

In any case, when we got engaged the following spring, we knew where to celebrate. We opened a bottle of Champagne, called our families, and got on the subway.

3

I don't know how I failed to mention it earlier, because it's absolutely perfect, but Brandon's first job was at Pizza Hut. He was fifteen, and he needed an after-school job, so he worked as a server at a Pizza Hut on New Jersey's Route 17. Lest you're hoping to pick up some insider tips for making those famous breadsticks or the Ultimate Cheese Lover's™ Pizza ("MADE WITH AL-FREDO SAUCE!" the ad copy screams), I should tell you that he never cooked there, though if he had, the work would have consisted largely of taking preformed pucks of dough out of a freezer.

From Pizza Hut, he moved up to TGI Friday's at the Palisades Center Mall, where he was also a server, hauling trays of Loaded Potato Skins, Parmesan-Crusted Crab Salmon (*Is it crab? Is it salmon?*), and Brownie Obsession®. He liked being a server. It wasn't always fun, admittedly: diners come to restaurants with expectations that are not necessarily based in reality. But because each table was different, each day was different, and the shifts went by quickly. Cooking in a restaurant, on the other hand, is repetitive by definition, and cooks never make the kind of money that servers do. Brandon had no interest in being a cook. The closest he came was a stint one summer in college, at a place called Pasta Amore, in Piermont, New York, where he was an expediter, a fancy name for the person who adds garnishes and makes sure orders are correct before they go out to diners.

While he was in graduate school, he did odd jobs for an uncle in New York City, buying groceries, running errands, and cooking the occasional dinner. Shortly after we met, that work began to taper off, so he got a serving job at Balthazar, the renowned brasserie in SoHo. You would think this was a great gig, but he was hired for the breakfast shift, which began at the punishing hour of 6:00 a.m., and he learned the hard way that he would be sternly reprimanded if he broke form for an instant, even for something as trivial as adjusting his eyeglasses.

By the time Brandon moved to Seattle in June of 2006, he was ready to be done with the restaurant industry. I didn't spend much time thinking about what our professional lives might look like in the years to come, but the rough plan, the logical plan, was that he would become a professor of music and I would write. There were, of course, his violin/boat dreams, but those were hobbies, after-hours projects. Ours would be a sturdy, quiet existence, the kind that involves corduroy blazers with elbow pads, couples yoga, and recreational bonsai cultivation.

But that was a long way off, and Brandon needed a job. He was starting a PhD program at the University of Washington that September, so he could only work part-time. We tossed ideas back and forth as we unpacked boxes, and one night near the end of that first week, we decided to celebrate his arrival by treating ourselves to a nice dinner out. I suggested Boat Street Cafe. Boat Street is known for its pickles (which are now sold nationwide; don't miss the prunes), and because Brandon is into pickles and vinegar (there were two dozen different bottles of vinegar tucked away in his moving boxes), I knew that he would like it. We ordered a starter portion of pickles, and what arrived looked like a painter's palette: a heap of turmeric-colored cauliflower, wedges of magenta beet, pale green fennel bulb, and a streak of tiny farm carrots, each bite bright enough to force my nostrils into an involuntary flare, the whole thing tamed with a pour of green olive oil. Sitting there at a slate table with a mossy tree branch jutting out of the wall above our heads, Brandon decided to come back with his resume the next morning.

I should specify that the resume Brandon took to Boat Street was for serving. It listed all the jobs I just told you about. But when Brandon introduced himself to Susan Kaplan, one of the two owners, she had just — as in, an hour earlier — lost a lunch cook. Her eyes locked onto the sentence that read, "Personal assistant for CEO in New York City: shopped for groceries, ran errands, cooked meals for a family of five." That was the only mention of cooking on the entire page, and of course, the CEO was Brandon's uncle. But Susan needed a cook, and Brandon was going to be it.

That afternoon, Susan called Brandon's references. The first person listed was his mother. Because she is an honest woman, she told Susan the truth: when Brandon cooks, the kitchen winds up looking like a pack of wild dogs has run through it. But Susan had an abundant supply of kitchen towels and bleach, and anyway, she liked that he was a composer. She would almost always hire an artist over a trained cook, she once told me, because artists have a keen sense for details: you can teach an artist to cook, but you can't always teach a cook to understand nuance and detail. She called Brandon the next day and hired him, and in doing so, she gave him not only his first cooking job, but a look inside a restaurant that was different from any he'd seen.

In some ways, Boat Street is an odd establishment. It has two chef-owners, Renee Erickson and Brandon's boss Susan, and they run two separate but adjoining kitchens. Susan runs lunch and catering out of one, and Renee runs dinner out of the other. The kitchens are a little haphazard, pieced together, soft around the edges, with spices in Mason jars and maps of France and a chipped enamel jug on the ledge over the prep sink.

"The nicest thing," Brandon told me after one of his first days there, "is that they have real silver spoons in the kitchen." Most restaurants have cheap stainless spoons for tasting, and the general feel is industrial, impersonal. Boat Street has good spoons and wooden cutting boards, stuff you would use at home.

The kitchens at Boat Street feel like places

where a person would want to spend time, where you could lean against the counter and have a glass of wine, where a home cook could confidently find her way around. I say this from experience, because I too worked there a number of times, filling in as a cook or a server for special events and catering gigs. The people who work at Boat Street want to be there, and not just because they get a paycheck. In most restaurants, there's a firm but invisible divide between the back-of-house (kitchen) staff and the front-of-house (dining room) staff: they interact little and generally like each other even less. But at Boat Street, the back of house and front of house were sometimes interchangeable. And whatever job you did, you got a share of the tip. Each day's tips were pooled, and a portion went to the kitchen staff. Before Boat Street, Brandon had never seen a dishwasher take home a tip.

Boat Street employees tend to stay, and to feel invested. If you wanted to learn how to do something in the restaurant — whether or not it pertained to your job — all you had to do was ask, and someone would show you. In the summer of 2008, when Brandon decided to try eating meat, he went to Russell Flint, then the sous chef of the dinner kitchen, and Russ taught him how to cook his first steak. (It is no co-incidence that Russ now owns and runs Rain Shadow Meats, the best butcher shop in town.)

I want to say that Boat Street feels like a dinner party. Between orders, the staff clusters in the kitchen, the way guests always do at a good party. There's a general sense that they know each other well, that they care for each other as much as they care about the food. And in the dining room, where upside-down parasols hang from the ceiling and a chalk drawing of Renee's late dog Jeffry watches over the bar, it's easy to feel like a part of it, to feel welcome, relaxed, and taken care of. But of course, I don't want to give you the wrong idea. There is a cosmic law, I believe, that requires every human on Earth to at some point consider, at least briefly, the idea of opening a restaurant, and that idea is usu-ally based on the mistaken notion that run-ning a restaurant is like having a dinner party every night. Most restaurants are not like dinner parties. Most restaurants feel more like Thanksgiving dinner.

Imagine that it's the fourth Thursday in November. You're making a dozen dishes for dinner, including some that are pretty complicated. You're standing up all day and for most of the night. You're worried about pleasing your in-laws, your second cousin, and a bunch of other people you wouldn't normally invite to dinner. You're rushing to get food on the table before the teething baby has a meltdown or before your grandmother's bedtime, whichever comes first. And once everything has been eaten, you have to clean up. No matter how much you love mashed potatoes and gravy and pumpkin pie, how much you love to cook, or how much you love to spray-paint gourds for a harvest-themed centerpiece, it's a lot of work. In a restaurant, you do that every day. At Boat Street, Brandon and his coworkers did that every day. But still, somehow, sometimes, Boat Street *did* feel like a dinner party.

Susan and Renee ran Boat Street on a human scale, with real respect, care, and a minimum of stupid rules. They made and sold the kind of food that they wanted to eat. They had figured out that working hard and living well did not have to be mutually exclusive — not even in a restaurant. It sounds simple, especially now that I'm writing it down, but it was a revelation for Brandon. Which is how, a little over a year after Susan hired him and only three months after our wedding, Brandon decided that he wanted to open a restaurant of his own.

SAUTÉED DATES WITH OLIVE OIL AND SEA SALT

These dates are one of my best back-pocket tricks because they're quick, elegant, and endlessly adaptable. At Boat Street, they're served as an appetizer, with olive oil and a good amount of crunchy salt to offset the sweetness. A few years ago, Renee opened a second restaurant, The Walrus and the Carpenter, and there they serve the same dates for dessert. You can also slice them, pit them, and serve them as part of a salad, ideally one involving oranges, pistachios, Parmigiano-Reggiano, and a soft, buttery lettuce. But I might like them best at breakfast, in a puddle of cold plain yogurt.

What follows is the basic method, not so much a recipe. Cook as many or as few dates as you'd like.

Olive oil
Whole dried Medjool dates
Crunchy salt, such as Maldon or fleur de sel

Place a heavy skillet over medium heat, and pour in enough olive oil to lightly film the bottom of the pan. When the oil is warm and runs loosely around the pan, add the dates, taking care not to crowd them. Cook, turning the dates frequently so that they heat on all sides, until they feel hot (careful!) to the touch. They should cook fairly gently; if they're taking on color, reduce the heat or turn them more often. Because of their high sugar content, dates can scorch easily, so keep an eye on them. You're just briefly warming and softening them, encouraging them to absorb richness and flavor from the olive oil.

Transfer the hot dates to a serving dish, and drizzle them with some olive oil from the skillet. Salt generously if you plan to serve them on their own, or only lightly if you're serving them in a salad or with yogurt.

4

One Friday afternoon a few months after he started at Boat Street, Brandon came to pick me up after work. I was still working at the publishing house, riding the bus downtown every morning, and I was surprised when he called at five to announce that he was waiting on the steps out front. I was even more surprised when I found him sitting next to a guy I'd never seen before, with short black hair and a broad grin. "This is Sam," Brandon said. "He started at Boat Street today."

Brandon was cutting back his work hours for school, and Sam had been hired as his replacement. Sam, as it happened, was also from New Jersey. Brandon was in charge of training him, and they hit it off immediately, talking music and pizza and the shared geography of their childhood (referenced, in proper New Jerseyan style, by turnpike exit number). Brandon offered him a ride home

51

at the end of the day, and they stopped to get me en route. That fall, in my off-hours, I'd been preoccupied with my first book proposal, which I was hoping to sell to a publisher soon. In the car that evening, Sam and I wound up talking about writing, and books, and about the nineteenth-century French poets that I'd been forced to read for my college minor and that he was somehow reading for the fun of it. Not long after, he invited us over for some of his excellent homemade tabouli, and that was how Sam became our mutual best friend.

One night, Sam took us to Cafe Lago, a restaurant where he'd worked a couple of years earlier. He had a feeling that we would like the food, and he wanted to introduce us to one of the owners, Carla Leonardi, who had become a friend. Sam's instincts were right on both counts. Dinner, which was delicious, included a very fine wood-fired pizza, and we enjoyed ourselves so much with Carla that we were there until the manager locked up for the night, long enough for a bottle of Carla's homemade *nocino,* or green walnut liqueur, to sneak onto the table. It was the first of many such nights at what became our designated corner table.

Carla was born in Italy but raised in Ohio,

and in the 1980s, she lived in New York. She knew New York pizza well. She'd eaten at Di Fara. When she and her then-husband, Jordi Viladas, opened Cafe Lago in 1990, it was the first restaurant in Seattle to serve wood-fired pizza, and most nights, Carla was at the oven. She'd recently been courted by developers who wanted her to open another restaurant, and they were offering to pay the construction expenses. She'd been thinking hard about it, thinking of saying yes, and of doing a new restaurant focused singularly on pizza. You can imagine, then, how often Sam and I lost her and Brandon to talk of tomato sauce, cheese, and dough.

Brandon was running some catering events for Boat Street at that point, and through one of them he'd met a prominent local businesswoman who was looking for a private chef for her family. Brandon offered himself, listing Carla as a reference, and it turned out that the businesswoman was a regular customer of Carla's restaurant. He got the job, and so began his first experience of running his own small operation, cooking dinner for the family three nights a week. Together we catered a birthday party for the businesswoman's husband, at which Stone Gossard, the guitarist of Pearl Jam, told us that he liked our pesto. I now see that I should have leveraged this fact into some kind of trade — the pesto recipe for Eddie Vedder's home address, maybe — but I was too busy blushing.

I remember Brandon telling me around that time that he'd been thinking a lot about Charles Ives, the renowned American composer. Ives sold insurance for most of his life and wrote music on the side. Because of his day job, Ives was never a "starving artist"; he made enough money that he could often give some to other composers, to help support their work. The further Brandon got into his PhD program, the more he began to think about Ives. He'd heard his composition professors complain about their lack of motivation to write, because they were burnt out on music by the end of the day. He watched other composers and freelance musicians fight to make ends meet, and he wondered if there was a middle path, à la Ives: maybe, if he didn't try to rely on music for a living, he might have a better chance of actually writing it in his off-hours, and of meeting with some success.

It wasn't that he was looking for a way to leave graduate school, but he was starting to question his reasons for being there. He liked teaching music, which is what his degree would prepare him to do, but he liked teaching high schoolers, not college students. One of his favorite parts of each week was Saturday morning, when he taught at the local conservatory for teenagers. He wouldn't need a PhD to be, say, a high school music teacher.

Around the same time, during the winter of 2006, I sold my first book. The publisher gave me a year to write it and an advance that allowed me to live modestly while I did, so I left my job in early 2007 and began work on the book full-time. I was elated and terrified. I'm the kind of person who likes order and routine, who needs to know exactly what is expected of her, when her next paycheck is coming, and where it's coming from. In other words, I am not a natural-born freelancer. I felt like the luckiest person alive, and like I might implode under the pressure. That Valentine's Day, Brandon surprised me with a midweek getaway to Portland, making the most of my newly liberated schedule. He skipped school, and we drove three hours down the interstate and ate our way through town. On the night of Valentine's Day, we went to Ken's Artisan Pizza, a place we'd both read about. We sat at the bar and ordered a couple of local beers and a starter of wood-oven-roasted Brussels sprouts. When our pizza arrived, he threw his hands in the air. "Why isn't there a place like this in Seattle?" he said. "Wood-oven vegetables, great pizza, good beer — we would eat there every week! We would eat there every day! We should open a place like this."

Brandon was always saying that kind of thing. I was getting used to it. I nodded in agreement, semi-absentmindedly. I mean, it *would* be nice if someone would open a restaurant like Ken's in Seattle.

I look at it this way: it's not illegal to think about committing a crime. You can think all you want. Things only get dangerous when you bring another person into it. You start having a conversation — *What time would we go into the bank? Would we wear ski masks or Reagan masks?* — and at some point you become guilty of conspiracy, even if you never actually do anything. That's because once you get two or more people in on a crazy scheme, it's a lot more likely to happen. You egg each other on. You find ways to sidestep seemingly impossible obstacles: security cameras, silent alarms, the fact that one conspirator has never owned a restaurant. Brandon thinks up a lot of crazy, and sometimes illegal, schemes.

I listen, and I might even nod, but my temperament is less Bonnie Parker and more Bea Arthur on *The Golden Girls.* He's thinking about a getaway car; I'm thinking that our hatchback is overdue for an oil change.

We got married in July of 2007. One night in October, over dinner at Cafe Lago, Carla and Brandon got talking about Pizzeria Bianco, the famous pizza place in Phoenix. They'd both been reading a spate of articles and awards lists that called it the best pizza in the United States, and maybe even in the world. They'd seen pictures of Chris Bianco's pizzas, and they were impressed. They started kicking around some ideas, guessing at Bianco's method and technique. Sometime between dessert and Carla cranking up Blondie on the stereo, a switch flipped. What came next was part joke, part boast, part dare, and all conjecture. With their powers combined, Brandon and Carla agreed, they could totally make pizzas like that. They could open a restaurant that would serve the best pizza anywhere.

5

Surprisingly, there was not an excess of alcohol involved. Some, but not a lot. We danced for a while in the now-empty dining room, hugged Carla goodnight, and when the next day came, the proposal was still on the table. Carla and Brandon were now opening a restaurant. I again nodded in agreement, semi-absentmindedly. They decided to meet in a few days to talk more about the idea, but I expected that would be the end of it. The restaurant would obviously go the way of the violin, the boat, and the ice cream shop.

They began to make plans. One night a week, they would meet at Carla's house to draft menus, talk potential spaces, and work out a budget. The possibility of a developer paying for construction was very tempting, though there was a catch to consider: the rent in that kind of scenario would likely be exorbitant, far above market value. But they had other options. Carla had some friends and regular customers who might be willing to invest in another restaurant of hers. The money would be there. They didn't have to worry.

Instead, they could work on the fun stuff, like scouring Craigslist for equipment. Right out of the gate, they found the restaurant-supply equivalent of a hundred-dollar bill on the sidewalk: a 30-quart Hobart mixer for only $900, about one-tenth the cost of a new one. They named it Sir-Mix-a-Lot.

While waiting for replies from Craigslist sellers, they began to test recipes. They were hoping to top their pizzas with house-made mozzarella, made from scratch — just milk, buttermilk, rennet, and salt. Most restaurants that "make" fresh mozzarella start from purchased curd, and the reason for that shortcut quickly became clear. Brandon and Carla made several batches of from-scratch mozzarella, some of which I was invited to sample, and most of which looked like cottage cheese. The pizza might be tasty, but you would have to eat it with your eyes closed. The mozzarella plan was shortly put on hold in favor of testing more crucial recipes, like pizza dough. I would come over at some point in the evening, and sometimes Sam would too, and we'd wrap up with dinner around Carla's dining room table. One night, I made a pot of creamy polenta, and to go on top, Carla braised a rabbit with herbs and crème fraîche. If ever you go into business with someone, make sure the deal comes with braised rabbit.

There's a strange culture among small business owners in Seattle. I can't explain it, and any attempt to do so makes it sound like even the businesspeople in Seattle are kombucha-brewing hippies (which, actually, some of them are), but by and large, small business owners here tend to cooperate rather than compete. They encourage each other. They genuinely — or it seems so, at least — want to support each other. For example, one night shortly before Delancey opened, when Brandon and I were there doing construction work, the owner of our neighborhood's other wood-burning pizzeria stuck his head in the door to give us a bottle of wine and his congratulations. He's since come in a few times to sit and chat, not seeming to mind that we're his main competition. (Yes, even people who own pizzerias enjoy going out for pizza.) And more importantly, Carla: she didn't have to encourage Brandon, but she did. He was an upstart who'd never even run a restaurant, much less owned one. She certainly didn't need him. She didn't have to team up with him. But she did.

At the time, there was starting to be a lot of talk in the food world about a place called Apizza Scholls, in Portland, Oregon. Earlier that year, the chef-owner had FedExed one of his pizzas to Ed Levine and Adam Kuban, the pizza-obsessed founders of the website Serious Eats, and they'd proclaimed it fantastic, even after its cross-country trek. For the sake of research, Carla and Brandon had to try it. I never refuse a good road trip, so one afternoon, the three of us got in the car and drove down for dinner.

Apizza Scholls was very, very good. The crust was so light and crackly that it almost seemed to fizz — Pop-Rocks come to mind, and that's a good thing — when you bit into a slice. It was something to think about. But it was only our first dinner of the night. Brandon also wanted Carla to try Ken's Artisan Pizza, the place we'd gone to the previous Valentine's Day. Ken's is, in a lot of ways, the perfect restaurant. The atmosphere is casual; the quality is high; and the prices are low enough that a person could easily become a regular. The space feels warm and comfortable, with tables made from old-growth Douglas fir that was once part of a roller coaster. The starters and desserts are great, and the wood-fired pizza is excellent, perfectly blistered at the edges. The place seats about sixty people, and it's consistently busy. People will wait for hours to eat there. We too took our place in line. Afterward, high on all of it and very, very full, we raced back up the highway and were home by midnight, with leftovers.

Based on what they'd seen at Ken's and what Carla knew from her own restaurant, they figured they'd need about 2,000 square feet, and that the project might cost around $250,000 if done on the cheap. But there were more calculations to do, and projections to hash out, and they needed professional financial help. That was when Brandon called my brother David. David is the youngest child from my dad's first marriage, and he's fifteen years older than me. We haven't lived in the same city since I was in diapers, but like any good older brother, he made sure to give me a nickname: Molson. It took me twenty-one years to figure out that my namesake was a brand of beer.

David has been in the restaurant industry since I was born. As a teenager, he was a cook in restaurants around Oklahoma City, where I grew up and he went to high school. After that, he went east to study at the Culinary Institute of America, and then on to Denver for a degree in hotel and restaurant management. Now he lives in Washington, D.C., where he and two longtime industry friends co-own seven restaurants. Most of their restaurants are big, handsome, polished places, the kind where you sign an important deal or go to brunch on Mother's Day. They make you feel taken care of. The staff is impeccably trained and the food consistently excellent. David doesn't sleep much, and it pays off. So Brandon called him up, and they talked shop.

David had good, sensible advice. *Pick a location,* he offered, *where other businesses are already succeeding; don't be the first gig on the block. Be sure that your concept mirrors the market, that it fits the location and the clientele. And make sure your debt base is broad by getting funding from a few different sources: a bank, investors, your own savings, and, of course, if possible, landlord construction funds.* In short, Brandon and Carla had some decisions to make.

By now it was January of 2008. They planned another research trip, this time to Pizzeria Bianco, to see what it was, exactly, that they were trying to equal. Like the trip to Portland, the one to Phoenix would be quick, just twenty-four hours and a lot of pizza.

A week after they bought their tickets, Carla and Brandon met for lunch. She had some difficult news, she said. She'd been thinking about the trip, about how she could go about getting her station covered at the restaurant and who would take care of her kids. It felt too complicated, too hard. An occasional overnight trip was not the problem; it was what would come after, what the trip pointed toward. The project had barely begun, but already, her time and attention were divided among too many demands. She didn't like shortchanging her family or her existing restaurant. Not only could she not go to Phoenix, she realized, but she couldn't open a new restaurant.

I was at home when Brandon came back from lunch and slumped into one of the kitchen chairs, red-faced. I'd never seen him cry before, and it scared me.

"You should do it anyway," I rushed to cheer. "You've already made it this far!"

"But I can't do it by myself!" Brandon cried.

"You'll figure it out. David will help you. You can do it, babe. You should do it!"

It's not that I thought, *I want you to open that restaurant!* As far as I knew, the project was another hobby, another way for Brandon to occupy himself between classes and work shifts and sleep. He'd get tired of it before long, and that would be the end of it. I'd always been frustrated by that pattern, because it's the opposite of my own. I rarely take on anything unless I've quietly and obsessively interrogated it, Vincent-D'Onofrio-on-*Law-&-Order*-style, and am certain that it will go the way I want it to. But all the same, I'd gotten used to Brandon, to who he is when he's absorbed in the Next Big Plan. I liked him that way. I loved him that way. It made him happy, so it made me happy. If he wasn't planning something, I wasn't sure who he would be. So I didn't think about what I was saying. I just said it.

Sometimes I think about what would have happened if I hadn't urged him to go forward, if I hadn't reassured him that he could do it. It's easy to wonder if I *made* him do it. But there's no use in speculating, because it's done. And I know that if I were to go back and repeat that afternoon, even with full awareness of what would come after, I would respond the same way.

He'd lost his co-conspirator, his veteran business partner, and his possible investors. He was inside the bank with a pistol and an empty duffel bag. He was the only one wearing a Reagan mask, but he was going through with it.

RICOTTA

Brandon and Carla never mastered mozzarella. But ricotta, on the other hand, is easy to make, incredibly versatile, and a very handy thing to keep around. The following recipe was developed by Brandi Henderson — more on her in a bit — and it's better than almost anything you can buy, particularly if you use the best-tasting milk and cream you can find. We use this ricotta most often on a white pizza, with fresh and shredded mozzarellas, slivers of garlic, and olive oil, but I also eat it frequently on toast, as an open-faced sandwich with roasted vegetables or stewed greens. When in need of a snack or quick hors d'oeuvre, I spoon ricotta onto crostini and then top it with a drizzle of honey, a pinch of lemon zest, crunchy salt, and black pepper. Another favorite crostino is ricotta topped with a small spoonful of marmalade and freshly ground black pepper. And for dessert, I like to roast rhubarb — a couple of pounds, cut into 3-inch lengths and tossed in a baking dish with half a cup of sugar, half a cup of wine (white or red), and a split vanilla bean, baked at 350°F for about 30 minutes — and serve it in bowls with a big spoonful of soft, cold ricotta.

If you plan to use your homemade ricotta

on pizza, drain it only until it's still very soft and spoonable. If you'd like to use it on crostini or a sandwich, you'll want to drain it so that it's a little more firm but still spoonable.

6 1/2 cups whole milk
1 1/2 cups heavy cream
2 cups buttermilk
1 teaspoon fine sea salt

In a Dutch oven (or other heavy pot with a capacity of about 5 quarts), combine the milk, cream, and buttermilk. Place over medium heat and cook, stirring occasionally to prevent scorching. Check the temperature of the mixture frequently with a candy thermometer, and when it reaches 180°F, stop stirring. Continue to cook until the curds and whey separate; the curds are the white clumps and the whey is the clear liquid. (You can gently drag a spoon through the pot, if needed, to see how the curds are coming along.) Remove from the heat, and set aside at room temperature for 30 minutes to allow the curds to strengthen.

Set a wide strainer over a large bowl or in the sink, and line the strainer with two layers of cheesecloth. Ladle the curds into the cheesecloth. (Do not press down on the curds, though I know it's tempting.) When all of the visible whey has drained out, the ricotta is likely the right texture for pizza: soft and creamy, but not soupy. If you'd like a thicker ricotta, continue to drain until it reaches your desired thickness. Stir in the salt; then taste, and add more as needed. Transfer the ricotta to a storage container, and refrigerate. Homemade ricotta will last for a week, but it tastes best within the first 3 days.

Yield: about 1 pound

6

Brandon developed his pizza with help, in a manner of speaking, from a composer who died two years before he was born. Her name was Nadia Boulanger — fitting, since *boulanger* is French for "baker" — and she was arguably the twentieth century's most influential teacher of music composition. Boulanger was famous for her memory: her students say that she had memorized every significant piece by every significant composer, from ancient to contemporary. She taught greats like Aaron Copland and Philip Glass, and one of Brandon's teachers at Oberlin Conservatory was a student of a student of hers. It was from this teacher that Brandon received a particular bit of advice, supposedly distilled from Mlle Boulanger.

It went like this: When you're looking to write a piece of music for, let's say, violin, you must first listen to as many other pieces for violin as you possibly can. You don't just sit down, tune in to your inner *artiste,* commune with your Muse, and write; you *research.* You study, asking why a given piece works the way it does, why the instrument itself works the way it does. Then, later, when you go to write your own piece, you have within you a library of sorts. You will know what is possible, where limits lie and possibilities exist, where you might fit in.

Even before Brandon and Carla hatched their big plan, he'd been doing informal research, searching for pizza that could equal what he grew up with on the East Coast. In Seattle, we ate pizza everywhere we could find it: Tutta Bella, Via Tribunali, Serious Pie, Pagliacci, Zagi's Pizza (now defunct), A New York Pizza Place (also defunct), general Italian restaurants with pizza on the menu. We'd gone to Portland, to Apizza Scholls and Ken's Artisan Pizza. We both have family in the Bay Area, so we drove down the coast and ate pizza at Pizzetta 211, Pizzaiolo, Zuni Café, the Café at Chez Panisse, and, in Santa Rosa, Rosso. In the summer of 2007, a few weeks before we got married, Brandon's uncle Tom asked if Brandon might be willing to fly to San Antonio on his behalf, pick up a car, and drive it to Los Angeles, and Brandon immediately said yes, because it meant that he could eat at Pizzeria Mozza, the much-lauded restaurant opened in late 2006 by Nancy Silverton and Mario Batali. Whenever we went to visit his parents in New Jersey, we'd sneak out for a weekend in the city, sleeping on an air mattress in a friend's studio apartment and spending the days racing from pizzeria to pizzeria: Totonno's in Coney Island, where the coal-oven pies were handsomely charred and Cookie, the surly co-owner, ruled over the dining room in frosted lipstick and white nurse's shoes; John's of Bleecker Street, whose wooden booths are covered in etched initials and hearts; Franny's, where the clam pie with chiles and parsley is a small-scale legend; Una Pizza Napoletana, where you could pay a hefty $21 for a twelve-inch Margherita pizza; and I could swear there were more than that, but you start to lose track at a certain point — unless you are Brandon, in which case, the time has now come to fly to Phoenix, to Pizzeria Bianco, to taste the most vaunted pizza in the country.

But Carla had pulled the plug on that, and now Brandon was on his own. He mentioned his disappointment to our friend Matthew Amster-Burton, and never one to miss an adventure that involves eating, Matthew invited himself along. "You can order more pizza this way," Matthew explained. He bought Carla's plane ticket, and on a late-January afternoon in 2008, they flew to Phoenix and went straight to Pizzeria Bianco, where a line was already forming out front.

Matthew was writing for *Gourmet* (R.I.P.) in those days, and he later wrote a short piece about their trip. "Like a martial arts student visiting the Shaolin Temple, my friend Brandon Pettit went to the mountaintop to gain wisdom from an acknowledged master of his discipline," he wrote. "The discipline is pizza, the mountaintop is Phoenix, and the master is Chris Bianco, chef-owner of Pizzeria Bianco."

They made the first seating at five o'clock and got seats at the bar, within view of the pizza oven, so that Brandon could study Bianco's technique. When Bianco slid the first pizza into the oven, Brandon measured the cooking time on a stopwatch and jotted it on a slip of paper. When their pies came out, Brandon produced a tape measure and took note of their diameter. I remember reading Matthew's story and thinking, *What's with all the details about Brandon taking notes?* By now, I was accustomed to eating pizza with a tape measure on the table.

Bianco's crust was crackly at the edges,

with a moist, elastic crumb. Compared to Di Fara, the gold standard to this point, the crust at Pizzeria Bianco was finer, chewier, with more bubbles around the rim. Its flavor was more complex, sweet with a whiff of sourness. As they left, Brandon went to thank Bianco, and the two of them got talking pizza, and then Bianco offered to meet up the following morning to talk some more.

Chris Bianco, it turns out, is into talking. What he's not into is trade secrets. His dough gets its flavor from a slow eighteen-hour fermentation, he offered. There's no magic to it. You can make great pizza in any oven, as long as it's hot enough. There are no pizza masters, he told Brandon. "I never set out to love pizza. I don't love pizza. I have no passion for pizza. I only love and I only have passion, so you fuckin' fill in the blank, I love it. If I was in Seattle I'd be smokin' fuckin' salmon or something." I should probably clarify that Bianco isn't originally from Phoenix; he's from the Bronx. He's true to a particularly earthy, New York City tradition of pizza — especially the part of that tradition that says, "Fuck tradition."

The truth is, Brandon didn't exactly do all of his research *first,* Boulanger-style. A person as thoroughly obsessed with pizza as he is will not be able to resist scratching the itch to make his own. Research and development happened in tandem, each feeding the other.

In the fall of 2006, a couple of months after we moved in together, I came home one evening to find him kneeling in front of the oven. He was trying, he said, to make it climb past its factory-set ceiling of 550°F to something more pizza-friendly, like 800°F. He'd set the oven to 550°F, and then he'd taken an old t-shirt, wet it under the tap, and draped it over the thermostat prong at the back of the oven, hoping to trick the machine into preheating longer. (He'd read about this trick from Jeffrey Steingarten, and yes, it came with a warning not to try it at home.) I arrived just as the high-heat grill thermometer he'd perched on one of the oven racks hit 700°F. The t-shirt began to give off an odor not unlike singed hair. I cringed. He looked at me like a kid who's just been caught drawing a masterpiece with Sharpies on his bedroom wall.

A year later, in the first weeks of their partnership, Brandon and Carla began to tinker with doughs, testing them in her wood-burning oven. They started with her restaurant's recipe — high-quality flour, water, salt, and yeast, fermented for about twelve hours — which yielded a very thin, crispy crust. But what they wanted was more bend and chew, something closer to Di Fara. They fiddled with the ingredients, adding and tweaking. Mozza uses a little rye flour for flavor, so they tried that. (They didn't like it.) Ken's Artisan Pizza uses flour from a Washington State cooperative called Shepherd's Grain, so they tried substituting it for Carla's usual flour. (They liked it, and Delancey still uses it today.) Christmas came, and we flew to New Jersey to see Brandon's parents. We went into the city, of course, and had lunch one afternoon at Di Fara. On a whim, Brandon asked DeMarco if he might let him buy a ball of his raw dough. DeMarco agreed. That night, Brandon stood hunched over his parents' kitchen counter, poking, stretching, dissecting, and finally tasting DeMarco's dough. It was salty, saltier than any of the doughs he'd made. But with sauce and cheese, the salt receded and the flavors fell into balance. The same way that he'd been taught to parse music — to break it down to its component parts, to pick out and listen to a single instrument amidst the noise of an orchestra — he began to teach himself to parse dough. When we got home, he and

Carla upped the salt in their recipe.

One night not long after, when he and Carla were mixing a new batch of test dough, they accidentally doubled the amount of water. The dough, if you could call it that, was more like wallpaper paste than a potential pizza. Carla wanted to throw it away, but Brandon suggested that they try baking it, just to see what would happen. After its twelve-hour rest, he shaped it and topped it as well as he could — it looked like Pizza the Hutt, from *Spaceballs* — and shoved it into Carla's wood-burning oven. The result was still a mess, but one corner of it, one lone corner, puffed and browned and bubbled like the pies at Pizzeria Bianco, and when Brandon tasted it, the texture was better than anything they'd done yet. So now, instead of adding ingredients, he began subtracting water, dialing back from the doubled amount until there was just enough moisture to yield big bubbles and good chew, but not so much moisture that the pie would morph into a space gangster.

With Carla off the project, Brandon was left to interrogate the dough on his own. He had a recipe with good texture and flavor, but compared to Bianco's, it lacked complexity. The charred spots on Bianco's pies tasted sweet, while the char on Brandon's tasted burnt, bitter. Remembering that Bianco's dough rises for eighteen hours, Brandon decided to try mixing a new batch of dough with less yeast, so that it would rise more slowly. The longer fermentation, Brandon explained to me, gave more time for the flour's starches to be converted to sugars, which meant that charred spots were actually tasty now, no longer reminiscent of blackened toast. He went on to explain seventeen other crucial facts about enzymes, microflora, and dough chemistry, which I will not share with you here. The upshot was, however, that the dough now had both a sweetness and a whispering sourness — a juxtaposition that could appeal to a composer or a dough chemist, and the kind of lasting flavor you find in a crusty loaf from a nice bakery. He had something he could work with.

Which is what he did. Spring and summer 2008 was the Season of Many Flatbreads. He made batch after batch of dough, jotting in a notebook each slight tweak in yeast amount and fermentation time. He watched YouTube videos on stretching and tossing pizzas and practiced in our kitchen, leaving every horizontal surface coated in a film of flour. He left the rounds of dough plain, with no toppings, so that he could taste their nuances, and he tried baking them in every oven, or makeshift oven, that he could get his hands on. He baked in our home oven — woefully still a mere 550°F — on a pizza stone that we'd been given as a wedding gift, on unglazed quarry tiles from Home Depot, and on the back of a large cast-iron skillet. He lined our gas grill outside with more quarry tiles, preheated it until it hit 750°F, and in half an hour of smoke and glory, succeeded in both baking a half-dozen spectacularly good flatbreads and completely draining the propane tank.

It became clear that he needed a proper wood-burning oven. So he put an ad on Craigslist, offering to exchange pizzas for the use of an oven. He got three responses, but when he went to check out the ovens, they were all too small, too haphazardly homemade, too Hobbit-like, to make for a good test. But Carla introduced Brandon to a woman named Ruth, and Ruth had a wood-burning oven in her backyard, which she offered up for his use. As it happened, her oven was made by the same company that Brandon had been considering for his eventual restaurant, which made it an ideal testing ground. Sometimes on Saturdays, after teaching his class of teens at the conservatory, he would spend the afternoon in Ruth's backyard, making flatbreads and pizzas — by now, he was happy enough with the crust that he'd begun adding toppings, too — until it was too dark to see. He made a simple sauce from whole canned tomatoes, zizzed up with an immersion blender and seasoned with kosher salt, dried oregano, fresh garlic, and a pinch of sugar. He tested brands of mozzarella, fresh and aged, and Grana Padano, aiming for a cheese pie that tasted like Di Fara's. Sometimes he even bought prosciutto. He didn't want to limit his pizzeria by making it vegetarian, but he also wasn't willing to serve something that he hadn't tasted. He began eating more meat, little by little.

Between pizza trials, Brandon worked on his business plan. First, the restaurant needed a name. He wanted the name to evoke New York, since his pizza sensibility is rooted there, but choosing the right word, or words, wasn't straightforward. Initially, he wanted a name that nodded quietly to Di Fara: maybe Avenue J (the street where Di Fara is located), or Midwood (its neighborhood in Brooklyn), or something related to the letter Q (the subway line that we took to get there). But this was when *Avenue Q,* the musical, was tearing up Broadway, and

Avenue J was too similar. And Midwood made our friends snicker, because our friends all have the sense of humor of a pubescent boy. And he couldn't think of anything interesting that involved the letter Q. One night after dinner, the two of us sat down in front of the computer and pored over a map of New York City, looking for the right word — a street, a subway stop, a neighborhood, anything. Brandon's eye landed on the Delancey Street subway station. It's not in a particularly picturesque part of Manhattan, but when Brandon was living in New York, it was a station that he particularly liked. It was always bustling, packed with people, and he passed through it often late at night, on his way home from visiting friends who lived on the Lower East Side. And we both liked the word Delancey itself: it felt classy and old-fashioned, like a pub lined with dark gleaming wood and frequented by old men with tweed suits and cigars. Not that the restaurant would include any of those things, but it felt right. (Though we do still quietly refer to Delancey by a couple of names that friends suggested: Mr. Pettiti's Perfect Pizza Paradise and Grotto, and Brandono's, for which Matthew wrote a catchy jingle — *pizza the way it ought to be, BrandOH-no's!*)

Now, with a name for the restaurant, Brandon began looking into funding. Without Carla as a partner, he would have to scale back. If the restaurant were smaller — say, 1,000 square feet instead of 2,000 — he could likely get a cheaper lease, and he'd need less money to open it and less equipment to run it. With help from my brother David, he wrote a business plan for a smaller, more modest restaurant, one that would cost between $50,000 and $75,000. (To put this in perspective, the national average for startup money required to open a restaurant is about $500,000, a figure that encompasses both holes-in-the-wall and fine dining establishments.) He called more than a dozen banks to inquire about small business loans, but this was mid-2008, and the economy was in shambles. None of the banks he called were giving startup money to risky businesses like restaurants. Our friend Olaiya, whom Brandon had met when they cooked together at Boat Street, offered another approach. Years earlier, when she was newly out of college, Olaiya bought a taqueria in Rhode Island, and she did it, she shared, by cobbling together small amounts of money from a lot of different people. Brandon could try the same approach.

This, of course, would mean going to our families and friends with his fantasy-slash-business proposition, a prospect that not only made the restaurant seem a lot more real but also made me very nervous. But I had to admit that I was proud of the work he was doing, and I trusted that David wouldn't let him do something totally stupid, so what the hell: the worst that could happen, and it would inevitably happen, I figured, would be that the restaurant never opened and we spent a few years paying back our parents and a few friends. It would be embarrassing — mortifying — and very expensive, and it might very well happen. But it probably wouldn't kill us. I might kill *him*, but it wouldn't kill us.

He went to our families first. His parents committed $5,000, and my mother threw in $3,000. A staggeringly generous friend offered the use of her credit card, which had a $24,000 limit. And after a lot of negotiating, our local credit union agreed to give him a $13,000 loan for the purchase of a wood-burning oven and a $15,000 line of credit. I was now in the awkward position of hoping that he *would*, in fact, open the restaurant, so that we wouldn't have to eat our words (and beans and rice for the rest of our lives), while also privately wishing that he would just hurry up and move onto the Next Big Dream.

It was June by this point, and I was busy revising the manuscript of my first book. The evening that I sent the final draft back to the publisher, we shared pizzas in Ruth's backyard and toasted with beers. We were both getting somewhere. He was happy. And I was happily distracted by the seemingly impossible fact that I had just written a book and was managing to make a career out of doing work that I loved. Until Brandon moved on to the next project, I was content to enjoy the pizza.

7

Brandon's first potential location for Delancey was an abandoned building with boarded-up windows on an overgrown lot underneath the I-5 Ship Canal Bridge. "It's classic mid-century," he breathed, "and it's *under a bridge*! Like Grimaldi's, in Brooklyn!" All of this is true, I can attest, though it would have probably needed half a million dollars in order to be inhabitable. Our budget was approximately a tenth of that. He went on to find and seriously consider three other spaces, two of which I toured with him and one of which I didn't, partly because Brandon had to stage something like a stakeout in order to even get inside, and partly because he worried that if I saw it, I would wind up in the fetal position on the sidewalk out front.

Some people can look at a house or commercial property and see potential beyond cobwebs and dark corners and stained ceilings; others, well, wind up in the fetal position on the sidewalk out front. I've worked hard on my potential-seeing capacity and have met with some success: a couple of years ago, I managed to fall in love with and now live contentedly in a small, bright 1958 house that Brandon found for us, with a deck that is partially rotting; a car-sized furnace that's half a century old; lipstick-red carpet and faux wood paneling over most of the first floor; and peeling paint on the garage doors, one of which no longer opens. We'll renovate someday, and that knowledge is somehow enough for me. But I am no Brandon. He's already making sketches of the roof deck he wants to build, once we've redone the current deck, revamped the heating system, renovated the first floor, and replaced the garage doors. He has what I believe is called *vision.*

In March of 2008, Brandon went on leave from his PhD program to work full-time on opening the restaurant. I greeted this decision with what might be described as pathological nonchalance. It made the prospect of the restaurant even more real, certainly, but there was still so much to do, so many problems to solve. It still might not happen. Anyway, I too am a PhD dropout, so who was I to question his decision? I knew what it was like to be staring down a future that you don't want and to decide to veer hard away from it, even if you're not entirely sure where you hope to go instead. I mean, I was supposed to be an anthropology professor, but here I was writing a book about food. Whether or not he finished school, I trusted that we would figure it out. Brandon would still teach at the conservatory on Saturday mornings and do catering and fill-in work for Boat Street, so our income wouldn't be affected. We'd be all right.

Brandon had just one requirement for his restaurant location: it had to be a one-story building. The pizza oven would require a chimney, and installing a chimney in a multi-story building would be prohibitively expensive. The first real potential location was in a neighborhood called Ravenna, just north of the University of Washington. On one of the main drags, there were two large adjoining storefronts for rent, with big windows facing a wide, shady sidewalk. We made arrangements to tour the units one afternoon, and our unnaturally helpful friend Susan, Brandon's boss at Boat Street and his newly appointed Oracle for All Things Business, offered to come along. It was a nice space, with a roomy dining area and some kitchen equipment already in place, which could save us a lot of money. But, as Susan pointed out, none of the cars on the street out front seemed to be actually *stopping;* they were all going somewhere else. The sidewalk was quiet. In the five years since we looked at the space, at least one other restaurant has rented it, moved in, and then moved on or died. As of this writing, it's for lease again. The Oracle knows.

Next up was the former Enterprise Rent-A-Car building on Roosevelt Way, in the University District. If you live in Seattle, you will know this building as the gray, graffiti-covered cube up the street from the former Giggles Comedy Nite Club (later, and also formerly, Jiggles Gentleman's Club). It's the place that's been for lease for as long as you can remember. When we were considering it, it was new to the market and still innocent of the graffiti to come. It did not yet have a pall of indifference hanging over the front door. Susan came with us to see it, as she did every space we toured, and we were all pretty excited about it. The day was warm and sunny, a rarity that will get any Seattleite's heart racing, but even I could see the potential.

The building was roughly square, with a narrow entrance in front, a large garage door next to the entrance, and between them a tall window. In back were two more garage doors, which opened onto a paved alley. It doesn't sound like much, because it wasn't: it was an empty shell made of cinder blocks. Save for a small office area in front, most of the space had been a garage. It had no insulation, an uneven concrete floor, and cobwebs as thick as the cottony fake ones people stretch around their front doors at Halloween. And because it was constructed from cinder blocks — which, as we stood there, I imagined crumbling like shortbread in an earthquake — it would require retro-fitting before it could be approved for use as a restaurant.

Now, all that said, when you cranked open the garage doors in front and back and let the daylight in, the place suddenly started to look very different. There were a half-dozen skylights scattered around the space, most of them covered in dead leaves, but with the garage doors open, you got a real sense for how bright, and even warm, it could be in there. It was open, loft-like, rough but inviting. With a good deal of scrubbing, strategic lighting, a couple of rugs, and some plants, it might even be charming — in a rough-hewn way, like a reclaimed industrial workshop. I now realize this is a lot like saying, *I could totally marry that guy, if only he had a job and didn't live in his mother's basement.* But if the rent was cheap, and if the landlord agreed to contribute to the cost of the retrofitting — not an unreasonable expectation — this could be the restaurant. When we got home, Brandon started doing research online and discovered, oddly enough, that the land on which the building sat had been, in the early history of Seattle, part of a plot called Pettit's University Addition. *It was fate! Brandon Pettit was destined to rent this building!*

Except that he wasn't. The landlord not only wasn't interested in helping with a retrofit, he was asking a monthly rate more than double the price of comparably dodgy locations, and he refused to negotiate. You could probably weave a nice, cozy sweater from the cobwebs in that place today.

But over the weeks during which the Enterprise space was slipping through his fingers — because it took a while to understand that the landlord really wasn't going to budge — Brandon found another possibility, a location about a quarter of a mile from our apartment, in Ballard. It was a building on Northwest 65th Street, just east of 8th Avenue, on a block populated by small neighborhood bars, a tattoo parlor, a hair salon, and a sneaker shop. We'd walked by the building dozens of times, wondering at the sign outside that read COOKIE CONSPIRACY. At one end of the building's face was a garage door, and at the other was a small storefront covered with signs: HOME STYLE COOKIES AND PASTRIES, CANDIE, and, in the window, C'EST MOO ICE CREAMS. The building was low-slung, mid-century, the lower half of its façade paved in long, narrow bricks and the top half a grid of rectangular windows trimmed in faded aquamarine paint. It looked like a small warehouse of some sort, but no one ever came or went, and the lights inside were rarely on.

One afternoon in May, Brandon decided to do some detective work. He went to one of the bars across the street from the Cookie Conspiracy building, ordered a beer, positioned himself in a seat by the window, and waited. By some miracle, his strategy worked: he spied an older man get out of a car, walk to the front door of the building, and go inside. Brandon leaped from his seat and went after him.

The man, it turned out, was the owner of the building, and within it, he operated a candy factory, making caramel corn and caramel apples. He also used the building to store an arsenal of equipment for making carnival food — funnel cakes, popcorn, and the like — which he rented out to other businesses. Actually, he didn't seem to be renting the equipment; he seemed to be mostly hoarding it — along with boxes of ingredients, boxes of paper bags, boxes upon boxes upon boxes. One corner of the large main room was set up as a commercial kitchen, with a stove and a ventilation hood and a giant mixer, and the ceiling was mottled with stains — from smoke, caramel explosions, who knows what. It was Willy Wonka meets *Blade Runner.* For this reason, I never personally went inside the Cookie Conspiracy building, though Brandon showed me pictures.

But if you could manage to look beyond the stacks of stuff, the stains, and the peeling paint, you could see that the candy factory would make a spectacular location for a restaurant: bright, airy, and with some of the most expensive parts of a commercial kitchen, like a stainless steel hood, already in place. It was walking distance from where we lived, on a busy neighborhood street with a loyal evening crowd. And as it happened, the owner had just purchased a large warehouse south of Seattle and planned to move his operation there in the fall, possibly via the Great Glass Elevator. The rent would be fair, and he told Brandon he would be out by October.

Susan, however, had reservations. She liked the space, but she worried about the owner. *He doesn't look healthy,* she told Brandon. *What if he dies?*

Brandon pushed on. He took measurements of the building, and he began to make plans. Summer came and went, and so did October, and so did November. The owner was renovating his new warehouse, and it wasn't ready yet. Brandon began to look at other locations. In early December, the building was still filled with stacks and piles. Brandon told the Cookie Conspiracy owner that he was moving on.

Sometime the following summer, around the time that Delancey opened, Brandon went for a beer at the bar where he'd held his stakeout, and the bartender told him that the Cookie Conspiracy owner had suddenly died not long before, the building still full of his equipment. The Oracle knows.

VIETNAMESE RICE NOODLE SALAD

During Delancey's gestation, and for a long time after it opened, we ate a lot of takeout. One of our favorite quick, cheap lunches was (and still is) a Vietnamese rice noodle salad called *bún,* and we like it enough that now, sometimes, we even make our own version at home. Don't be put off by the number of steps. The dressing, a take on *nuoc cham,* can be made a few days ahead, and if you've got the ingredients on hand and the dressing prepared, you can bang this meal out in very little time.

This salad is wide open to adaptations and a great vehicle for using up leftovers or odds and ends. Take the recipe and run with it, using whatever vegetables and cooked meats you have on hand. Here are some tips to help as you go:

- Slivered raw carrots are a must, I think, as are sliced cucumbers. A small handful of each is about right. Another essential ingredient is salted peanuts. It's a sad day when I go to make this salad and discover that we have no peanuts.
- You'll also want some sort of crunchy lettuce or raw cabbage-type vegetable. Thinly sliced romaine is nice, as are

the smallest, crispest leaves of more tender green lettuces. Napa cabbage leaves, sliced crosswise, have a great watery crunch, and baby bok choy works beautifully, too. Whatever you use, a handful per person is a good bet.

- Blanched snow peas, sliced thin, are always welcome. Start with a small handful.

- Bean sprouts, the white ones that are about as wide as spaghetti, commonly show up in Vietnamese noodle salads, although I could do without them. It's up to you.

- Fresh herbs! Sliced basil or Thai basil is delicious here, as is chopped cilantro. A few sliced mint leaves isn't a bad idea, either.

- If you really want to do it up right, fry some shallots: Peel and thinly slice a few shallots, pour oil into a skillet to a depth of 1 inch, let it get nice and hot (between 275° and 325°F), and, working in small batches, fry the shallots until they're light golden brown. Transfer to a paper towel to drain briefly; they'll crisp as they cool. Fried shallots are one of the tastiest toppings for *bún,* albeit fiddly to make at home. I'll tell you a secret: If you happen to have a can of French's French Fried Onions in your pantry, try tossing some of those into the salad instead. Pretty tasty.

- As for protein, it's hard to mess up. One of my favorite meats for this salad is a leftover pork chop, sliced, but grilled or sautéed shrimp is a close second. Slices of cold steak are delicious, too, and for vegetarians, extra-firm tofu, cooked almost any way, is great. This salad is also a good place to use up leftover roasted chicken, although I recommend tasting a piece with the dressing before committing; not everyone likes the union of chicken and fish sauce.

- And though it changes the whole concept, try substituting hot freshly cooked rice for the noodles. We do that often. I like to use Calrose, an inexpensive Japanese-style medium-grain rice that's grown in California and commonly sold in Asian grocery stores. (Or if you live on the West Coast, you can probably find it in ordinary grocery stores, too.)

Lastly, note that this recipe doubles nicely.

For the Dressing

3 tablespoons fish sauce

3 tablespoons freshly squeezed lime juice

2 to 3 tablespoons (25 to 35 g) light brown sugar

6 to 8 tablespoons water, to taste

1 medium clove garlic, minced

1 fresh Thai (also sold as "bird's eye") chile, minced

For the Salad

8 ounces (225 g) thin rice noodles (roughly the width of linguine)

3 or 4 napa cabbage leaves, thinly sliced crosswise

1 medium carrot, shredded or cut into matchsticks

Half a cucumber, halved, seeded, and thinly sliced

A handful of chopped fresh herbs, preferably a combination of basil, cilantro, and mint

8 ounces (225 g) cooked meat, cut or torn into bite-sized pieces (see note, above)

1/2 cup (65 g) salted peanuts, coarsely chopped

To Prepare the Dressing

In a jar or small bowl, combine the fish sauce, lime juice, 2 tablespoons of the brown sugar, 6 tablespoons of the water, the garlic, and the chile. Whisk well. Taste: If it's too pungent add more water, 1 tablespoon at a time. If you'd like more sweetness, add more brown sugar, 1/2 tablespoon at a time. Remember that you're going to be putting this dressing on unsalted vegetables and noodles: you want the dressing to have a lot of flavor, but it shouldn't knock you over. Pour into a serving bowl. (Covered and chilled, the dressing will keep for 3 days to a week.)

To Assemble the Salad

Bring a large pot of water to a boil. Add the rice noodles, and cook for 4 to 5 minutes, until tender but not mushy. Immediately drain the noodles into a colander, and rinse them well with cold water. Lay out a clean kitchen towel on the countertop, shake the colander to drain away excess water, and then spread the cooked noodles on the towel to drain further.

Divide the noodles between two or three good-sized bowls, depending on the number of diners, and top with the vegetables, herbs, and meat. Scatter the peanuts on top. Allow each person to spoon on dressing to taste. Toss well, and eat. (Alternatively, you can present this salad family-style: Toss the vegetables, herbs, and noodles in a mixing bowl and then mound them on a serving platter. Arrange the meat over the noodles, and top with peanuts. Each diner can scoop their own portion from the platter and dress it as they see fit.)

Yield: 2 to 3 servings

8

Our friend Ben is one of those people who can cook anything without breaking a sweat. I love him for that. I also hate him for it. In his off-hours, he's often cooking, and it's usually something from the canon of French classics, the kind of dish that comes with not only a formal title, but a formal title in italics. The phone would ring at eight on a Wednesday night, just as we'd be starting to scramble some eggs for dinner, and it would be Ben, calling to invite us over for *coq au vin, steak frites,* or *truite amandine,* his tone so casual you'd think he were talking about opening a can of soup.

"There was a special on trout at Ballard Market today," he'd say, "and I'm about to make a cocktail. Why don't you come over?"

We'd go over. Ben is an opera director, and he and Brandon have known each other since Brandon was in college and Ben was dating Brandon's friend Bonnie. In early

2008, he landed a job as the assistant director of Seattle Opera. He moved to town that summer and found a little house to rent in our neighborhood, on Alonzo Avenue, about a mile from our apartment. We'd let ourselves in the side door, and he'd be waiting with his signature cocktail, an icy pour of gin spiked with freshly ground black pepper and a clove of raw garlic. Then would come the trout: a whole fish for each of us, crisp-skinned, dressed in browned butter, sliced almonds, and parsley. And in case the sight of a sautéed whole trout wasn't enough to make us giddy on a weeknight, this specimen would be sitting upright on the plate, folded in half using some classical technique so that its tail poked jauntily through its mouth. I want you to know that it takes a lot of restraint to keep from putting a half-dozen exclamation points at the end of that sentence. Ben would even have warmed the plates.

If Ben hadn't moved into that house on Alonzo, I doubt Brandon would have found the building where we opened Delancey. But one day that fall — probably early November, though none of us can remember the date — Brandon stopped by to see Ben, and when he couldn't find a parking space on Alonzo, he drove up the block to

Northwest 70th Street, took a right, and parked outside a charming old one-story commercial building with a FOR LEASE sign in the window.

When Brandon came home later and told me about it, I remembered the street fair I'd gone to on Northwest 70th that summer, with Ben. The block between Alonzo and 14th Avenue had been closed to cars, and the businesses there had propped their doors open and put chairs and tables out on the sidewalk. There was face painting, and a bouncy castle, and there must have been a petting zoo, because I remember a small, straw-lined pen in front of what is now the dining room of Delancey, with a goat and maybe a pig? Honoré Artisan Bakery, which sits right next to Delancey, had just opened, and we bought some of their pastries. This block was technically in my neighborhood, but I'd never realized there were businesses there; I'd thought it was all bungalows for blocks around.

The FOR LEASE sign, as it turned out, had gone up only the day before Brandon saw it. There were three adjoining storefronts on offer. The landlord showed us into 1415, which only shortly before had been the Peapod Book and Birth Store. Straight ahead, about eight paces from the front door, was a wall with a mural of Winnie the Pooh and Christopher Robin and, between them, a quote by A. A. Milne. If you turned back to look at the door, you'd find a second mural above it, this one of a couple of three-masted ships, sails billowing, on a baby-blue sea. Walking toward the Winnie the Pooh wall, you'd pass through a doorway into a second room in back, where there was a psychedelic rainbow-painted plaster cast of a pregnant woman's belly hanging on the wall. From that back room, you could turn right and wind up in a low, dark rabbit warren of a hallway that led to a small bathroom on the left and, on the right, a doorway into the rear of number 1417, formerly Gracewinds Perinatal Services. There, just inside the doorway, was a closet. If you opened it, you were rewarded with the sight of a bumper sticker on the wall that read, MOMS ROCK! AT KEGELS. (I figured this was just a triumphant, if oddly punctuated, statement of fact. But the other day, I learned that there is, or was, a Ballard-based mommy-punk band called The Kegels. Their 2005 album *Totally Effaced* includes tracks like "Sux2b3" and "Mini-Van Mom.") And then, going back into the hallway, you could continue on to 1421, which had already been claimed, the landlord told us, by a woman who planned to install an umbrella shop. This made me feel better about the odds of the restaurant succeeding. I mean, if you think a lot of new restaurants fail, imagine the death rate for umbrella shops.

Common wisdom (and my brother David) says that you should open a restaurant in a part of town where there's plenty of traffic, plenty of street life to support it. You should open in a part of town where similar businesses are already succeeding. You should probably not open a restaurant on a street like Northwest 70th in Ballard, where no one will see it unless they're looking for it. The street is narrow and relatively quiet, punctuated by speed bumps, and it's easily a fifteen-minute drive from downtown Seattle. When I moved to Seattle in 2002, I didn't know anyone who lived in Ballard, and people talked about it as though it were far enough away that it might as well be the island on *Lost.* But we'd stumbled upon a nice little duplex to rent there in 2006, and we'd gotten to know the area. We liked that it felt like its own small city, that it had a lot of independent businesses, that it looked out for its own. Brandon's restaurant could be a true neighborhood joint there, hidden in plain sight on Northwest 70th. It could be the kind of place we'd like to have around the corner from our apartment.

Together, 1415 and 1417 added up to just over a thousand square feet. In that kind of space, the restaurant could seat about forty people — a little smaller than the other potential locations, but it felt right. (Many more people than that, and he might be taking on more than he could manage; many fewer, and he wouldn't make enough money to be worth the effort.) There was plenty to tackle: 1415 had wall-to-wall carpet; 1417 had a lumpy teal concrete floor; both had ugly cottage cheese–like popcorn ceilings; and the façade was a queasy mash-up of beige, green, blue, and bright red. But the important parts were there. The ceilings were high. A dozen saucer-shaped industrial pendant lights hung from the ceiling on a network of steel tubes. They were exactly the kind of thing we liked, old but timeless, and even in a salvage shop they would have been expensive. Here, they were included in the deal. The bar across the street had a loyal following, and the bakery next door was getting a lot of press, and the café diagonally across the way had just been bought by a young chef who planned to serve an ambitious all-local menu, all the way down to the sea salt. Everything about it felt right, including the fact that 1417 had once been a tavern, a small but notable detail that made it likely that the city would approve permits for a restaurant.

And in a previous incarnation, number 1415 had been a violin shop. If a man can't build a violin, he might as well make pizzas in a former violin shop.

THE BENJAMIN WAYNE SMITH

It seems only fitting to include a recipe for our friend Ben's signature cocktail — and to name it after him, while I'm at it. I've watched him make it many times, but for our purposes, I asked him to write down his method. This is what he gave me:

I was spoiling myself, dining at the Palena Cafe in Washington, D.C. The café is attached to a very fancy and expensive restaurant (Palena), which one can see at the end of the long hallway connecting the two. It's sort of like looking into first class from coach.

Anyway, I sat alone at the bar one night eating spaghetti and veal meatballs and overheard a man in a cowboy hat order his martini like this: "Take the cheapest gin you have, crush a garlic clove, add a few grinds of black pepper, and shake with ice. Strain it into an 'up' glass. Take the clove from the shaker and add it to the glass."

Try it with three ounces of gin. You can adjust the garlic quotient by more or less crushing of the clove. Obviously, the more pepper you use, the sharper the drink. I usually do two big grinds on a very coarse setting. It floats in the drink, but I don't mind.

I usually use Burnett's gin when I make this cocktail, but anything cheap will do just fine.

NOTE: Ben is going to give me a royally hard time for this, but contrary to his advice, we usually use Voyager or Tanqueray. And we use less gin per drink, about 2 ounces. Rinsing the glass with dry vermouth isn't a bad idea, either.

9

There are approximately one million steps between signing a commercial lease and opening the doors to the public. Anyone with a regular heartbeat can probably tell you that. Before Delancey, when I considered someone who had successfully navigated those steps — my brother David, say — I assumed that he had been able to do it because he had a gift, possibly bestowed upon him at birth, that gave him a bunch of skills that non–business owners don't have. There was a Business Fairy, a cousin to the Tooth Fairy, and she'd visited him in the nursery and, with a wave of her wand, gave him The Knowledge.

When Brandon signed the lease for the space that would become Delancey, I wanted to know where the hell that fairy was. It was November 21, 2008, the Friday before Thanksgiving. He had two empty storefronts, and because the landlord had given him six months of free rent, he hoped to turn them into a restaurant within that amount of time, if not sooner. I was around, but I wasn't formally helping: I was paying our bills with freelance writing work, and my book would be published in early March, consuming the bulk of my time for weeks before and after. Anyway, though the signing of the lease certainly seemed to mean that Delancey was happening, I still couldn't imagine it. I could say to you, *My husband is opening a restaurant,* but the words didn't mean a lot to me. I still couldn't see how, exactly, he was going to do it. The construction alone was an enormous obstacle, and I couldn't see beyond it. Brandon is a bright, resourceful guy, but there was a lot to learn — and I'm just talking about construction, not management or marketing or even making pizza.

In the early weeks of planning Delancey, Brandon thought he would *hire* the Business Fairy. Most people building businesses (and homes, and everything in between) do. She's called a contractor.

Brandon met with three contractors who came highly recommended. The first was too busy. The second gave a bid for $250,000, about four times Brandon's total budget. The third gave a similar bid, but then he leaned in and confided, "You know, you don't *really* need a contractor. You can do this on your own. Hire an architect to help you with the permits, but you can do the rest."

So it was that Brandon mostly built Delancey himself, with a mishmash of paid, traded, and volunteer help. The team consisted of a local architect named Henry Walters; my architect-designer cousin Katie Caradec and her friend and business partner, Pantea Tehrani, who worked remotely from the Bay Area; one of the landlords, who doubled as a discount plumber-slash-construction-worker; our friend John Vatcher, who gave us his toolbox and his weekends; various employees at home improvement stores, who offered advice; and nearly two dozen other assorted friends, who were compensated in Cool Ranch Doritos. Together, they got the job done, if not quickly, easily, or elegantly. Construction began in early December of 2008, and if we're going to be perfectly honest, it's still going on.

The first thing Brandon bought was a box of surgical masks. Then the Winnie the Pooh wall came down, and after it, the plaster cast of the pregnant belly. Then he ripped out the carpet, and then the popcorn ceiling. There's no quick way to scrape a hard, bumpy crust from a surface eight feet above one's head, but he devised a couple of decent tools, the most effective being a long broom handle with a putty knife screwed onto the end of it. (Don't worry: he had the popcorn ceiling tested for asbestos first.) The process took a week, because as it turns out, a person can hold a tool above his head for only a certain amount of time before his shoulders relocate semi-permanently to the level of his ears. Between episodes of scraping, he'd pick out toilet fixtures or fill out paperwork for permits. When he'd come home at the end of the day and draw himself a bath, there'd be a half-cup of ceiling in his hair.

By the time he'd finished scraping the ceiling, the debris on the floor was thick enough that you could drag your foot through it and spell out SOS or, if you spanned both rooms, MAYDAY MAYDAY MAYDAY. After Brandon carted it all to the dump, it was time to do unspeakable things to the floor.

What we wanted was a natural concrete floor: no paint, no nonsense, just a coat of sealant. Concrete floor we had, but it was riddled with nonsense: glue, foam padding residue, and teal paint. So, at the recommendation of a Home Depot employee, Brandon rented something called a shot blaster.

A shot blaster looks like a large vacuum cleaner, and it's a cross between that, an industrial sander, and a tennis ball machine. You push it (slowly and with difficulty: it's heavy) across a flat surface, the same way you would a sander. As you do this, it pummels the surface beneath it with tiny steel balls, which it instantly sucks back up and recirculates, and the abrasive action of the balls strips away paint, glue, sealant, skin, whatever they encounter. The shot blaster rental fee was steep, and Brandon only paid for twenty-four hours, so he had to work fast. He had appointments all day and couldn't start until after dinnertime, so I went along to help. Because only one person can push the machine at a time, I passed the hours — we were there until after midnight — by cutting out paper snowflakes and sticking them to the front windows with electrical tape. It was almost Christmas.

The shot blaster easily removed the blue paint, the carpet glue, and the foam residue, but it also left a conspicuous pattern in its wake, like the trail a lawnmower leaves on grass. Had we been told that it would do this, we would have shot-blastered in a pretty crisscross pattern, country club–style. As it was, what we had were wobbly stripes that pointed roughly in the direction of the eventual pizza oven, Brandon's spot in the kitchen, as though to say, *The guy to thank for this design atrocity is standing right here.* Worse, the process had revealed some substantial cracks and an old floor drain in what would be the dining room, problems that had been hidden, sealed with concrete, until we blasted the crap out of them. We looked at each other, and suddenly he was Tom Hanks and I was Shelley Long and we were in *The Money Pit.* At any moment, a bathtub was due to fall out of the ceiling.

And that is why the floor at Delancey is painted.

At the end of a day of shot blastering or other hard labor, nothing tastes better than a meatloaf sandwich. I like mine as straightforward as they come: a slice of meatloaf, mayonnaise, and bread. Maybe lettuce, but probably not.

This recipe is not about reinventing meatloaf. For the most part, its ingredients are classic ones, though when they come together, I think the result is particularly good. My subtle tweak to the concept is fish sauce. You might think a typically Asian ingredient seems out of place in something as American as meatloaf, but at my friend Matthew's suggestion, I tried it, and I love the quietly deeper, more savory flavor it brings. You won't actually taste the fish sauce itself, but you'll benefit from it.

Whenever I have a day-old baguette or other French-style bread, I make breadcrumbs for recipes like this one. Trim away and discard the crust; then tear or cut the bread into 1-inch pieces. Pulse the pieces in a food processor until they're reduced to crumbs roughly the size of barley or short-grain rice.

And a note about the meat itself: Don't be tempted to buy the leanest possible grade of ground beef or pork. You want some fat for tenderness.

Lastly, your hands are your best tool for mixing meatloaf evenly and quickly. My favorite mixing technique is something I call "the Claw," and it's described below. If the thought of a handful of raw meat makes you squeamish, try keeping a box of powder-free latex gloves in the kitchen.

1 tablespoon olive oil
1 medium (about 250 g) yellow onion, finely chopped
2 cloves garlic, chopped
1 1/3 cups (about 65 g) fresh breadcrumbs
About 1/3 cup (80 ml) whole milk, or enough to saturate the breadcrumbs
1 pound (450 g) ground beef
1 pound (450 g) ground pork
1 teaspoon fine sea salt
2 teaspoons fish sauce
2 large eggs, beaten well
2 teaspoons Dijon mustard
1/3 cup (10 g) minced fresh Italian parsley
1/3 cup (85 g) ketchup, plus 1/4 cup (65 g) for topping the loaf

Preheat the oven to 350°F. Line a rimmed baking sheet with parchment or aluminum foil.

Warm the oil in a medium saucepan over

moderate heat. Add the onion and garlic, and cook, stirring occasionally, until the onion is softened and translucent but not brown. Set aside.

Put the breadcrumbs in a small bowl, and drizzle the milk over them, stirring to moisten. Set aside.

Put the beef and pork in a large mixing bowl, breaking up any large hunks. Add the salt, fish sauce, eggs, mustard, parsley, and 1/3 cup ketchup. Add the onion and garlic. Using your hand, squeeze the milk from the breadcrumbs; then add the breadcrumbs to the meat mixture (discard the milk). Holding one hand in a claw shape, press it down into the ingredients, and briskly stir with your hand to mix evenly. When the meat and seasonings are uniformly mixed, pick up the mixture and turn it over in the bowl, and briefly mix again. (Turning it over helps to ensure that no ingredient settles to the bottom and clumps there.)

Transfer the mixture to the prepared baking sheet, and use your hands to pat and shape it into an approximately 9 by 5-inch loaf. (If you find that the mixture is sticking to your hands, rinse them well and leave them slightly wet; the moisture will keep the meat from sticking.) Brush the loaf evenly with the remaining 1/4 cup ketchup.

Cook for 45 minutes to 1 hour, or until a thermometer inserted into the center of the loaf reaches 155° to 160°F. Cool for at least 20 minutes before slicing.

Yield: 6 to 8 servings

10

It took almost twenty-four hours to build the wood-burning oven, not including the hour spent breaking into a semi.

Brandon could have bought the oven fully assembled, but getting it into the building would have required removing at least one of the two plate glass windows that surround the front door, and possibly a wall. Instead, he bought the oven in parts. And to make sure that he didn't completely botch its assembly, he paid to fly in somebody from Mugnaini, the maker of the oven, to help. (Somehow, that was *still* cheaper than removing and replacing the window.) His name was Michael, and Brandon picked him up at the airport one night at the end of February. The next morning, a semi with two giant crates inside pulled up at the curb on Northwest 70th Street, and that's when the excitement began: the back of the truck wouldn't open.

They jiggled the appropriate handles. They pressed all available buttons. They tried to pry it open with a shovel. The driver announced his hypothesis: the cargo had shifted to lean against the door and was now keeping it from opening. So he restarted the engine, gunned the truck fifty yards up the street, and then abruptly slammed on the brakes, hoping to whiplash the cargo forward. That didn't work. Someone brought over a tire jack. Using the shovel, they managed to wedge the tire jack under the door, and with a crack and a squeal, the door reluctantly slid up.

Inside, in addition to the two crates filled with oven parts, was a ship's mast — which, as it turned out, had been the source of the cracking sound. It had been wedged diagonally into the truck, and it barely fit, so the slightest bump in transit could have caused it to shift, lean into the door, and pin the door down. I assume the freight company had insurance, but to the seafaring Seattleite who received a broken mast: We owe you a pizza.

In any case, once the door was open, they could lower the first crate to the sidewalk. That was easy. But the second crate — the one containing the six-inch-thick concrete-and-sand floor of the oven and the metal legs it stands on — was too wide for the lift gate. So they had to unpack the crate inside the truck and then lower the unprotected oven floor, teetering with each inch. They could then move it into the restaurant, using a piano dolly and a hydraulic hand truck that Brandon had rented the day before. Unfortunately, the floor and its metal stand were welded together, and they were too wide for the front door of the building. In order to fit, the entire 800-pound structure had to be turned onto its side, laid on the hand truck, and shimmied through the door. Brandon ran up and down the block, recruiting anyone he could find, and it took five of them — Brandon, Michael, the owner of the bakery next door, the owner of the café diagonally across the street, and a biblically unlucky friend who happened to stop by with a book for Brandon — to get it into the restaurant.

This all took a few hours. Then Brandon and Michael went to Home Depot for bags of refractory cement, perlite, and tools. It was time to build the thing.

The first task was to lay the hearth tiles, a dozen thick clay panels, on top of the floor of the oven. Once the hearth was in place, the arch at the mouth of the oven could be set, and then a domed ceiling could be built above it. The dome was made of wide, curving panels, like petals from an enormous stone tulip, and there were five panels in all, each weighing 200 pounds. They nestled against one another, each slightly overlapping the next, and on top went a final round panel, the crown. Getting the crown settled properly requires some maneuvering, and the best bet is for someone to army-crawl into the oven's maw, turn onto his back, and, looking up, wiggle the crown into place. Michael had done it once on a previous job, and had gotten so anxious that he rushed to get out and broke a rib. So Brandon did it. I missed this part, and I am grateful for that, because I imagine it looked a lot like that scene at the end of *Jaws* when the professional shark hunter is eaten alive.

Once the dome was built, its seams were covered over and sealed with a spackle-like layer of refractory cement, a special type designed to endure high temperatures. By this point, it was around midnight, and a drunk from the bar across the street had wandered over. Grabbing the doorway to steady himself, he announced that he knew how to build wood-burning ovens, and that Michael and Brandon were doing it wrong. He was escorted back across the street. Then the entire dome was wrapped in ceramic fiber, and then it was enclosed in metal walls. Then began the cement mixing, which Michael taught Brandon to do by hand, kneeling on the floor over a bus tub, with a surgical mask, industrial rubber gloves, and a folded-up cardboard box under his knees for cushioning. "It's like making pasta!" Brandon reported triumphantly: You dump a bag of powdered cement into the tub, make a well in the middle, pour in some water, and begin stirring from the center out. They did that a few times, or maybe a dozen times, because who could keep count, and then that cement got dumped, along with some perlite, on top of the dome, for added thermal mass and insulation. When that was done, Brandon drove Michael to his hotel, and then he came home to apply some thermal mass to his sore back. He now had a pizza oven.

Meanwhile, my book was coming out the following week, on March 3rd. I was at home during most of the oven-building, out of my mind with excitement and anxiety, fielding e-mails and making last-minute arrangements for my book tour. More than ever, I was in Book Land; Brandon was in Pizza Town. Most of our conversations around that time went approximately like this:

Molly: [Blah blah blah] the book.

Brandon: [Blah blah blah] the restaurant.

Molly: [Blah blah blah] book. [Blah blah blah] book tour.

Brandon: [Blah blah blah] restaurant. [Blah blah blah] pizza.

Molly: I'm sorry, what were you saying?

Brandon: I was talking about the restaurant. What were you talking about?

We laughed at ourselves and made light of it. I knew that Brandon was supportive of my work, that he wanted to hear about it, even if he was distracted. I wanted to be supportive in return. Or maybe I wanted to *seem* supportive. I wanted to be the kind of person who would applaud her husband's hard work, even if the end goal scared her. He had asked nothing of me but my support. But in truth, I mostly wanted the restaurant to go away.

In any case, when I arrived with my camera the next morning, the oven was done. It was like magic, magic that leaves a dusting of refractory cement mix on every surface. Brandon and Michael had built the oven in the center of the room, because that's where there was space to maneuver, but now, that morning, we had to move it to its proper location against a wall in the kitchen. And the move had to happen before eight o'clock, when the ventilation company would arrive to build the chimney and roof vent. This part of the story did not involve any magic, but rather me, Brandon, and Ben, still in pajamas — pajamas and leather jacket for Ben — inching the 3,600-pound beast across the room on the hydraulic hand truck.

The way the kitchen was laid out, the oven had to be positioned at a precise angle. Basically, we had to set it down at the correct point along the wall, and then turn it thirty degrees away from the wall. I'm sure there must be a tool that makes this easy, but we did not have it. The tool we had was a plastic protractor, the kind you use in high school geometry. I found the flattened cardboard box that Brandon had kneeled on to mix the cement, and I measured a tiny thirty-degree angle in one corner of it, extending the lines to make a large triangle. Then I cut it out, and while Brandon and Ben wiggled the oven around on the lift, inch by inch, I held the cardboard wedge between it and the wall, until they touched.

Then Ben left to get dressed for work, and the ventilation people came, and I went back to Book Land.

SRIRACHA-AND-BUTTER SHRIMP

Ballard, our neighborhood, is the historic center of Seattle's Scandinavian fishing community, and the waterfront is still very active. (For you *Deadliest Catch* fans: Ballard is where a number of the show's boats spend the off-season.) Delancey isn't on the water, but it has customers who are commercial fishermen, and occasionally they bring by their latest catch. We made this dish for the first time using spot prawns caught by one of them.

Brandon and I got the idea for this recipe from a feature in *Bon Appétit.* A number of chefs were asked about their favorite uses for sriracha, the rusty-red hot sauce with a rooster on the bottle, and a chef named Sean Baker gave a brief description of a shrimp dish. Brandon riffed on Baker's outline to cook dinner for us on a night off, and it's become one of our favorite hot-weather meals. All you need to go with it is a loaf of crusty sourdough, a bottle of cold white wine, and a roll of paper towels. (Your hands are going to get very, very messy.)

For this recipe, you'll want raw shrimp in the shell without their heads on. (Or, if you can get some with heads, even better! But they can be tough to find.) Shrimp are sized by how many it takes to make up a pound, and for this recipe, we like 21–25 or 26–30 shrimp (meaning that there are 21 to 25, or 26 to 30, per pound), also labeled "large." Oh, and if you live in an area where you have access to spot prawns, by all means, use them instead.

Lastly, this recipe doubles well, serving four to six.

3 tablespoons (42 g) unsalted butter
1/3 cup (80 ml) sriracha
2 large cloves garlic, minced
1 pound (450 g) large shrimp in the shell (see head note)
1 1/2 teaspoons grated lemon zest
1 packed tablespoon minced fresh basil
1 packed tablespoon minced fresh mint

In a 12-inch skillet over medium heat, melt the butter. Add the sriracha, and stir to blend. Add the garlic, and cook for 3 or 4 minutes to soften its flavor. If you taste the garlic at this point, it should no longer taste raw. Add the shrimp, and raise the heat to medium-high. Cook, stirring occasionally, for 5 to 7 minutes, until the shrimp shells turn pink and the flesh is just cooked through but still tender. (If necessary, cut into one with a sharp knife to check for doneness: the flesh should be opaque, not translucent.) Add the lemon zest, basil, and mint, and toss to mix well.

Serve immediately, and be sure to set out an empty bowl for discarded shells.

NOTE: If you use spot prawns in this recipe, their shells will likely be pink when raw, so you'll have to test for doneness by checking the flesh only.

Yield: 2 to 3 servings

11

With the oven built and installed, the central axis of the kitchen was now in place, which meant that Brandon could turn his attention to everything around it, like the industrial dishwasher, or the plumbing for the three-compartment dish sink, the prep sink, the two floor sinks, the mop sink, and the hand sink. Commercial kitchens are 90 percent sink. Brandon suggested that I write a post for my blog about this phase of construction, and that I call it "Sink or Swim." He writes all my best jokes.

Most of the kitchen at Delancey is visible to diners, but to hide the refrigerators and storage shelving behind the wood-burning oven, Brandon built a wall along the oven's face, essentially concealing everything but its mouth. Actually, he built the wall twice: once somewhat casually and imperfectly, since it wouldn't be load-bearing, and a second time after an inspector gave him a hard time for it. With instruction from our friend Rebecca (the only master teacher of Pilates who also offers lessons in tiling and grouting for the price of a few cold Coronas) and her ex-husband, John (a saint who was at that point helping Brandon with construction work nearly every weekend), Brandon then covered the wall in brownish-gray rectangular "seconds" — slightly flawed tiles, sold at a discount — from Heath Ceramics in California. Sam came to help one day, and under the last tile, up in the highest corner on the left, they slipped a piece of paper with their names and the date.

Brandon is an avid thrift-shopper, and from the day that the restaurant was conceived, he'd been thrifting for supplies. There were about a dozen secondhand stores that he combed each week, and he devised strategic routes between them to minimize traffic and driving time. "I'm hitting the north loop," he'd tell me one afternoon, and I'd know that he was starting at the Ballard Goodwill and would finish a few hours later at the St. Vincent de Paul in Kenmore.

Between late 2007 and the spring of 2009, when construction became a full-time job, Brandon brought in enough loot to fill two basements and approximately one-sixth of two different garages. Early on, he and Carla had bought Sir-Mix-a-Lot, the used thirty-quart Hobart mixer. Because it was too heavy to get down the stairs to the basement of our duplex, they stashed it in her garage, which already bulged with backup supplies and equipment for her own restaurant. Meanwhile, our basement was also growing a restaurant supply–induced gut. One corner was heaped with boxes, more than a dozen of them, filled with bowls, gratin dishes, and ivory-colored plates of every size. A shelf in another corner held skillets, saucepans, stockpots, lids, aluminum mixing bowls, two blenders, and three blender jars. On the floor was a cardboard pizza box stuffed with mixed-pattern silverware, purchased on eBay; a stereo receiver; two sets of speakers; and a pair of light fixtures for the bathrooms. To get to the washing machine, you had to pass through an obstacle course of cast-iron table bases. And what couldn't be crammed into our basement was crammed into our friend Olaiya's: more table bases, dozens of restaurant-grade food storage containers, and, for a while, the six sinks. All in all, Brandon spent nearly $10,000 — a good portion of his income from Boat Street and teaching, minus his share of our rent and bills — on secondhand equipment.

The previous spring, in April of 2008, our neighborhood's historic bowling alley had closed after more than fifty years in business, and there was an auction to sell off the furnishings and fixtures, down to the wood floor of the bowling lanes. Brandon went, and he came home with more than a dozen teak Thonet chairs. It was the buy of the year. But he had nowhere to store them — Delancey didn't yet have a location — so our friends Shauna and Danny offered to keep the chairs in their garage. As it turned out, the chairs sat there for more than a year. One Saturday in the spring of 2009, that spring of construction, we rented a truck and brought them to Delancey. With our friends Matthew and Laurie, a pack of sponges, and three dented dinner knives, we relieved them of chewing gum and tobacco residue. Before that weekend, I hadn't known that cigarette smoke could, over half a century, harden around an inanimate object just like Magic Shell ice cream topping.

Now my first book was out, and that kept me busy. But when I was around, I would help where I could. Most of the time, this meant meeting Brandon at the restaurant in the early evening, when it got too dark to do construction work — he had only a couple of industrial clamp lamps to see by — and acting as his prep cook while he made test pizzas. He'd cured the oven — a multiday process of firing it to increasingly high temperatures — and now he could start actually cooking in it. He'd learned a lot about cooking with fire from Carla, and from tinkering in Ruth's backyard, and from YouTube videos of Chris Bianco, but now he had his own oven to get acquainted with. And with a working oven and a workable dough, it was also time to think about the menu and to test topping combinations. Thus began the period of our lives in which we ate pizza three to five nights a week — a period that I should, in fact, speak of in the present tense, because we're still in it. Our diet is the envy of seven-year-olds worldwide.

The menu was something that I could help with, and despite my doubts, I wanted to. In our relationship, though we both cook, I've always been the main menu-planner, the one with a knack for piecing together the components of a meal so that they make sense, like a jigsaw puzzle. I like doing it. When Brandon wrote his business

141

plan, the sample menu was the one section where I could make a contribution. Serving as Chief Menu Consultant, we decided, would be my role at the restaurant. When I announced on my blog, in late November of 2008, that Brandon was opening a restaurant, I wrote, "But I will be there too, helping where I can, and the menu is a real combination of his style and mine. It is inspired by two of our favorite restaurants: Zuni Café in San Francisco, and Boat Street Cafe. It happens, yes, that the emphasis will be on pizza, but there will also be wood-fired vegetables from local farmers, seasonal salads, charcuterie, and rustic desserts, the kind I like to make at home." We wrote four seasonal menus for the business plan, with starters like halibut cheeks with brown butter, corn, and cilantro; or a salad of shaved fennel with aged Gouda and Asian pears; a pizza topped with salt cod brandade and slow-roasted tomatoes; another pizza with caramelized ramps, Gruyère, and bacon; and for a summery dessert, roasted apricots with almond cake and house-made mascarpone or, in the spring, roasted rhubarb with orange zest and fresh ricotta.

It was a given that Brandon would do a cheese pizza based on the flavors of Di Fara's, with tomato sauce, a little fresh basil, and a combination of fresh mozzarella, aged mozzarella, and Parmigiano-Reggiano or Grana Padano. Most New York–style pizzerias use only aged mozzarella, the kind you grate or shred, on their basic cheese pie; Di Fara's was the first he'd known to add fresh mozzarella, too. The result was soft and milky in some bites, rich and chewy in others, and perfectly salted, and though it had a decent amount of cheese, it somehow wasn't gloppy or soggy. Brandon's basic cheese pie would use the same three cheeses — two mozzarellas and Grana Padano, because Brandon likes it better on pizza than Parmigiano-Reggiano — and as a nod to Di Fara, we decided to call it the Brooklyn.

It was New York that got him into this, but Brandon also wanted to serve a Margherita, Italy's classic cheese pie. It's simple: just tomato sauce, fresh mozzarella, fresh basil, and olive oil. That also means that it's hard to do well, because there's nowhere to hide an unbalanced sauce or a cheese with so-so flavor. He would make a Margherita, but he had to get it right.

Beyond those preliminary decisions, there were a lot of details to work out. Do you grate the aged mozzarella, or do you grind it to small pebbles in the food processor?

Do you slice the fresh mozzarella, do you hand-tear it into pieces, or do you put it in the food processor, too? How much of the sauce and cheese can you use before your pizza leaks a pool of orange oil and requires blotting with a half-dozen napkins prior to consumption? And does the basil go on before or after baking?

That said, the toppings were never the point for Brandon. The point was the basic combination of crust, sauce, and cheese, and the way they talked to each other. When most of us think about pizza, we might think about pepperoni or goat cheese or ham and pineapple, but what makes pizza *taste like pizza,* what allows us to recognize this particular food as pizza, is the union of crust, sauce, and cheese. When Brandon started to think about what kind of pizzas he would make, his focus was on those elemental parts. He wanted each component to be the best it could be, and he wanted those components to be in balance. The menu would have an interesting seasonal pizza or two, but for the most part, he didn't want to devote a lot of attention to elaborate toppings, because it took enough attention just to assemble and bake each pizza — at slightly different temperatures for different toppings — so that the textures and flavors would be exactly as he wanted.

So the Margherita would be the restaurant's nod toward Italy, and the Brooklyn would be the foundation for almost everything else. If you ordered a Pepperoni, for instance, you were essentially ordering the Brooklyn plus pepperoni. The same went for the Padrón, which was a Brooklyn with roasted fresh chiles. But you could, of course, order a Margherita and ask to have pepperoni or padróns added to it. Nobody was going to tell you that you couldn't eat what you wanted to eat. The menu wouldn't *encourage* diners to add a metric ton of toppings, but Brandon would be happy to do it, if asked.

(The current record for most toppings added to a single pizza was set on January 22, 2011, by a man who must have spent the day skiing or snowshoeing or maybe just smoking a lot of weed, because he had worked up an appetite that could be satisfied only by a Pepperoni with added sausage, prosciutto, bacon, pickled peppers, and double the normal amount, he specified, of crimini mushrooms.)

The opening menu would also have a couple of sauceless pizzas, like the Zucchini Anchovy, a typically Roman combination of zucchini blossoms, anchovies, and fresh mozzarella, only our version would use thinly shaved zucchini in place of the blossoms. And there would also be the Crimini, which was based on a Jamie Oliver recipe that we liked to make at home: a platter of thinly sliced mushrooms, fresh mozzarella, fresh thyme leaves, and olive oil, slipped under the broiler until browned and bubbly and then eaten with bread. Brandon would swap out the platter for pizza dough and the broiler for the wood-burning oven.

But that spring, while the oven was only half-tiled and the basement filled with stuff, the toppings were still in their testing phase. We didn't know yet whether anyone would even like the Crimini, because Brandon was still trying to figure out how much mozzarella to put on it. There was a folding card table at one end of what is now the bar, and it, with a clamp lamp hooked to the side, was my prep station. I had a cutting board, a paring knife, a box grater, a plastic pack of fresh thyme sprigs and a bag of crimini mushrooms, a tub of fresh mozzarella, and a few tester bottles of olive oil that we'd been given by a vendor eager for a contract. I'd slice mushrooms and pick thyme leaves, and once there was enough for a few pizzas, Brandon would do his part. A batch of dough made about forty pizzas, so we'd be there until midnight. There wasn't enough room on the folding table for the finished pizzas, so after a while, once we were done sampling them, we'd stack them on the rungs of a nearby ladder. It wasn't so much about the eating, anyway. It was about practice and repetition, about taste memory and muscle memory, about trying to figure it out.

WINTER SALAD WITH
CITRUS AND FETA

I don't think it's possible to get tired of pizza. (I do, though, reserve the right to reverse my stance in a few years.) But regular infusions of salad and crunchy vegetables help to make us feel less like grade-schoolers at a slumber party.

Salad is no easy feat in winter and early spring in Seattle, when grocery store options are slim and there's no lettuce at the farmers' market. But a few years ago, I discovered that I love escarole, one of the sweeter, milder members of the chicory family, and shortly after that, raw kale became the It Thing, and suddenly cold-weather salads seemed a lot more plausible. Brandon came up with the following citrus-based dressing one January at the restaurant, where it's served on chicories with French feta, citrus segments, and plenty of chopped pistachios. When it's on the menu, I eat it a few times a week, and when I make it at home, I also add avocado slices.

I've intentionally left the salad ingredient amounts open to interpretation, and you should feel free to use a combination of whichever greens you like best. You'll want a good handful per person. For the grapefruit segments, I like to add them with a light hand, but you might like more than I do. Don't skimp, though, on the pistachios or the feta.

For the Dressing

1 tablespoon Champagne vinegar
1 tablespoon freshly squeezed orange juice
1 tablespoon freshly squeezed grapefruit juice
1/2 tablespoon freshly squeezed lemon juice
1/2 clove garlic, pressed or grated on a Microplane
1/8 teaspoon fine sea salt
Pinch of freshly ground black pepper
Pinch of grated lemon zest
Pinch of grated orange zest
1/4 cup (60 ml) olive oil

For the Salad

Mixture of winter greens, such as escarole, lacinato kale, endive, and radicchio
Grapefruit segments
A generous amount of unsalted pistachios, coarsely chopped
French feta, crumbled
Avocado, sliced (optional)

Prepare the Dressing

In a jar or small bowl, whisk together the vinegar, citrus juices, garlic, salt, pepper, and zests. Gradually add the olive oil, whisking to emulsify. (This dressing will keep in the refrigerator for a few days; after that, the citrus juices tend to oxidize.)

Assemble the Salad
Combine the greens in a wide bowl and add dressing to taste. Toss gently, and top with grapefruit, pistachios, and feta. Add avocado slices, if using, and serve.

Yield: about 1/2 cup dressing, enough for about six to eight servings of salad

12

It occurs to me that when I write about Delancey, I sometimes toss around possessive pronouns a little carelessly. Sometimes it's *his* restaurant; sometimes it feels like *ours.* Sometimes it sounds like I'm right there next to him in the construction debris, and sometimes it sounds like I'm reporting from a safe, tidy newsroom, keeping tabs on him via satellite phone. None of these is incorrect. Even while I lived and ate and worked and slept beside a man who was clearly opening a restaurant, for a long time I tried to pretend that the restaurant didn't exist.

When the idea for Delancey was hatched, I was so deep in my first book that I was writing in my sleep. I'd wake up and *boom!* have a new paragraph. The book was my full-time job, and when that was finished, I had freelance work, and then it was time to revise the book, and then it was time to get out and promote it.

Let's say your spouse is a statistics professor and you're a biologist. If you made a Venn diagram of your professional interests and capacities, the circles might overlap, and they might even overlap quite a bit, but still, you're the biologist and your spouse is the statistics professor. You have different jobs. Brandon and I were like that. What made our Venn diagram odd was the fact that most of my writing has been about food. Our circles don't just overlap; they're nearly consuming each other.

So I should explain why, in the beginning, I didn't want to be a part of the restaurant, and aside from the menu planning, I didn't really even want to help with it.

At first, Brandon had Carla. The restaurant belonged to *them. They* were opening a restaurant. It wasn't my project. But after Carla pulled out and I slowly began to help now and then, I knew that Brandon found it odd that I was so hesitant, that I wasn't more interested, that I even seemed somewhat threatened by it. But he told himself that I was just preoccupied, nervous about my own work, and that wasn't an inaccurate assessment.

He knew the restaurant would be a lot of work. He had no illusions: *of course* it would be a lot of work. But he had done the math, and he believed that it would be worth the trouble. It's not that I didn't believe him; I just wasn't wholly convinced. He began planning the restaurant at almost exactly the moment that the U.S. economy began to tank. By the time the lease was signed, the unemployment rate was soaring and businesses were keeling over left and right. Here he was, opening a type of business with a notoriously high failure rate in the middle of the worst recession since the Great Depression. Plus, Brandon has never been great with numbers. He'll accidentally reorder a sequence as he jots it down, or he'll dial a phone number backwards. Still, *even knowing that,* I didn't want to look closely at his calculations. I didn't have time, I told him. I could help him with the menus, because that was squarely up my alley, but that was all. I didn't want to open a restaurant. And hey, we were talking about a giant, violin-shaped ice cream boat. Why should I waste time on the details?

But I couldn't say that to Brandon. Instead, I put my head down and did my own job, and because I like to see Brandon happy, and because I knew how much he wanted the restaurant, I encouraged him to keep doing his job, too.

■ ■ ■ ■

Publishing a book is the headiest experience I can imagine, short of waking up one morning to find myself in bed with Bruce Springsteen circa *Born to Run.* I got to buy some new clothes and dress up and leave the house a few times — strange behaviors for a writer — and best of all, I felt like a *professional.* I loved meeting the people who had supported me and my writing, who had made the book possible. I felt like somebody.

So I wasn't prepared for what came after: a sadness like I had never experienced. When I got home from my book tour at the end of March, the high lasted for about a week, and then, without being able to say why, I felt empty. I've since been told that there's a kind of "postpartum" depression that can come with finishing a large creative project, and that it's normal, but at the time that it was happening, I didn't know any of that. I just knew that I felt used up. I felt paralyzed, stuck — unsure of what to do next, unable to even *think* about what to do next. The rational part of me knew that I was probably just exhausted, wading through the gray zone of transition from one project to another, but that's not what it felt like. I couldn't feel anything.

This was also when I began to understand that the restaurant was, in fact, going to open. This was not a hobby, another project that Brandon would get bored with and forget. I began to add it up: He had built a pizza oven. He owned a thirty-quart industrial mixer. Our basement was filled with equipment. He was actually doing it. While I was busy with my own work, it had been easy to avoid thinking about the future, about this nebulous restaurant thing. But once the book was done, there was nothing else to think about. It was right there in front of me. I chose this moment, four months after the lease was signed, to tell Brandon for the first time that I didn't want him to do it.

I had never expected us to have nine-to-five work lives, the kind where you come home, have dinner on the table by six-thirty, and then sit on the couch with a glass of wine and watch *Law & Order* reruns until bedtime. (I prefer to watch *Law & Order* reruns in bed, on the laptop, with a box of Trader Joe's chocolate Joe-Joe's cookies.) I chose to write for a living, and that is not a steady, reliable, nine-to-five gig. While my line of work does give me a lot of day-today flexibility, the work itself is not easily contained or compartmentalized, and the hours are rarely regular. In spite of that, I had expected our lives to have a gentle rhythm. I expected us to eat dinner together at our kitchen table, the way we had in our first years as a couple, the way my family always had. I expected us to get into bed together, at the same time. I expected the peace of mind that comes with having at least one member of the family — Brandon, I thought — receive a regular paycheck from an outside employer.

"I don't want you to own a restaurant!" I blurted out. We were at home, in the kitchen, cleaning up after lunch. I couldn't hold it in anymore.

"What are you talking about?" Brandon said, stunned. He stared at me.

I didn't want anything that a restaurant stands for. I didn't want him to work nights and holidays. I didn't want to eat dinner alone. My interest in food has always been about sharing it — about the kitchen table, about home cooking, not restaurants. I like the intimacy, the quiet, the scale of home cooking. During college, I tried interning in the kitchen of a highly regarded restaurant in San Francisco, an internship I was very lucky to get, and though the word *hate* would be too much, I didn't care for it. I loved that it was my job to get up to my elbows in food, but I didn't like the most basic fact of it: it's not like home cooking. When you plate a dish in a restaurant, you hand it to a server, and that's the end of that. It's time to plate another dish, and then another, and then another, and you'd better do it fast. There can be an appealing badassery, and even a certain romance, to being a line cook, but it's not part of the job description. Mostly, you're sweating in a hot kitchen, and the dining room — the eating part, the pleasure part, the connection part — is on the other side of a wall. It's grueling, repetitive work, and you do it while most of the world is relaxing. The customers are not there to share a meal with you, and anyway, you haven't got time: there are a dozen tickets on your rail.

"I don't want a restaurant!" I was screaming now. "I don't want this! I never wanted this!"

"Why didn't you say something?" he screamed back. "Why didn't you tell me?" We were both crying. "You *encouraged* me!"

"I didn't think you would go through with it! I thought it was just a thing — a hobby!" I cried.

"It was never a hobby!" His jaw tightened.

"How could you think it was a *hobby*? I did this for us! I did this for you! I did it because I thought we would both like it!"

The restaurant was already doing what I feared it would. We had recently watched the stresses of restaurant ownership tear up a friend's marriage, and I figured it was naïve to expect anything different for ours. The restaurant industry runs on long days, late nights, and regular infusions of adrenaline, alcohol, and drugs. It's not a family- or marriage-friendly atmosphere; it's what gave us Anthony Bourdain's *Kitchen Confidential*. I didn't want Brandon to become a Restaurant Person, a guy in a stiff white coat who answers only to "Chef" and yells orders in broken Spanish while snorting coke with waitresses (or off of waitresses) during dinner service. I didn't want to lose the person I knew.

Brandon tried to reason with me. The restaurant would change things, he agreed, but it would be for the better. We'd be able to stay in Seattle, which would not likely have been the case if he'd stayed the course and gotten his PhD: he'd probably have wound up an assistant professor of music at the University of Faraway Town We Would Only Agree to Move to Because There Were No Other Options on Earth. He might actually make good money from the restaurant, too, which would definitely not be the case with a university teaching job. Anyway, pizza, he assured me, is a recession-proof food. People will always want to eat pizza, the same way they'll always want hamburgers and barbecue. It was a no-fail business proposition. He also knew his intentions for the restaurant: that it would feel as close to a dinner party as he could possibly make it, a place like Boat Street, a restaurant for us non–Restaurant People.

"If we don't like it," he said gently, "if it doesn't make us happy, I'll sell it. Give it five years, and we can sell it."

The following week, I went to a therapist that a friend recommended, and all I could do was sob about how overwhelmed I was. I could see that the therapist was sort of scared for me, or possibly *of* me. He told me to take some time off work, to give myself a break, and afterward, he sent me a bill for $300.

When the therapist recommended that I take a break, he was probably envisioning naps and hot baths. But I needed something to do. I didn't want to write: I had nothing to say and, as far as I could tell, probably never would again. But standing still didn't feel any better. My husband was moving forward, and the longer I stood there, or lay in the bath, or whatever, the more the shape of us as a couple would stretch and contort. I knew that my reluctance to get behind the restaurant was tantamount to a decision. I didn't want my life to change. That was it: *I didn't want my life to change.* But it already had. I hated that.

But it's why, in mid-May, I began to help Brandon with the construction full-time. I still wanted no part of actually operating the restaurant, but now that I wasn't writing, I could at least *think* about the restaurant without getting the shakes. I could see that if he was right, if this business was going to make it, he needed help. I needed something to do, and he needed someone to do it. By this point, we were also running low on money and the restaurant's first rent check would be due soon. The clock was ticking: the restaurant had to hurry up and open, so that it could start making money. Getting to that point, however, would take more hours and sweat than one person can produce. So we started a new routine: each morning, Brandon and I would go together to "the space," as we called the restaurant before it began to look like a restaurant.

I had been using a lot of emotional energy

keeping even the thought of the restaurant at arm's length, so it surprised me now to find that it felt good to give in to it, to let myself be pulled along by something so tangible. I was relieved to find that it was nothing like writing. I could put my whole body into it. It was like wading into the ocean at night. I couldn't see farther than my own hand. I knew I had to jump in, and I chose to jump in, but it was *dark* in there. We moved by feeling our way. We swept, and we cleaned, and then we hauled equipment, and then we opened a bag of Cool Ranch Doritos, and then we finished the bag of Cool Ranch Doritos, and then something got installed, and then something broke, and then something got fixed, and on it went. It began to be *our* restaurant.

Though we wanted to open within a month, there were still piles of insulation and rubble in the corner, and neither the floor nor the walls were painted. Even the furniture needed attention, because most of it was salvaged, which is shorthand for "an amazing find, but it'll eat through an entire package of steel wool and sponges and an afternoon of scrubbing before you can safely use it." There were also concrete tabletops to build. There would be eleven of them in all, and each would require a bag of dry concrete mix, a gallon of water, and a lot of sweat. Brandon did the mixing by hand, the way he did when he built the oven, and I helped by filling pitchers of water, dumping them into the mix, and cheerleading. When the consistency was right, he'd pat the wet concrete into a mold. The next day, he'd unscrew the sides of the mold, and then we would gently lift out the concrete slab. When it was fully dry, I would smear it with seven coats each of two types of sealant. Then Brandon would wiggle each slab into its own steel frame (thankfully not made by us; that's what metal shops are for), and then the whole thing would be glued to a piece of plywood, and then the plywood would be screwed to a salvaged table base. After we'd done that eleven times, it was hard to *stop* doing it, so we mixed a double batch and made a top for the bar.

Once we'd swept up the concrete dust, it was time to paint. We wanted the restaurant to look minimal but not cold, so we chose a warm white for the walls. No one mentioned that we should consider using a primer to cover the mural of the ships above the front door, so even after four coats of paint, they sail proudly on, toward the dining room and eternity. We disguised them with an acoustic panel.

I had never experienced anything as consuming as those days. It was as all-encompassing as my post-book letdown had been, but where that was like a fog with no visible boundaries or end, I could at least see that this construction process would stop at some point, even if it wasn't until the day before we opened. I could *do something* about the restaurant. I could push it forward. I could move with it. Sometimes I would get a glimpse of what the place might look like in the end, when it was full of noise and people and the oven was full of fire, and it would make me so proud and excited and terrified that I didn't know whether to grin, or sob, or both. And the afterglow of that feeling would light the way through the dark for a while, until I got a glimpse again.

In late June, my cousin Katie and her friend, Pantea, the team who designed the restaurant, came to help with the final details. As a thank-you, and so that Brandon could get some practice on the wood-burning oven, we cooked dinner for them. Olaiya and her boyfriend came, and Sam, and Ben, and we sat under a row of lights that Katie and Pantea had fashioned from old cider jugs, at a big wooden table that Brandon and I had carried home from Goodwill in the rain three years earlier, thinking that we might someday use it in our dining room. Now it was in our restaurant. Sometime between plating wild arugula salads and slicing Brandon's pizzas and washing what felt like eight million dishes, I realized that I was having a very good time. We were feeding a roomful of our favorite people, giving them a good night. I felt like a part of the place — the walls, the floors, the old loaf pans we used for storing the silverware. I remembered something that Brandon had said a couple of months earlier, after I had told him that I didn't want him to open the restaurant, after we had stopped screaming. He told me that even though I couldn't see it yet, Delancey would embody everything that mattered to us. (Actually, I can't remember his exact words, and nobody but Steve Urkel whips out *embody* in spoken English. But that was the gist.) That night in June, for the first time, I believed him.

The restaurant had taken away what control I thought I had over our marriage and our future, and after I was done denying the fact that there was a restaurant at all, the only thing to do was hang on. I decided to stop thinking so hard. I decided to get in the middle of it. After that dinner in June, I decided to try working in the

166

kitchen at Delancey. It might not be forever, but I wanted to try. I'd been helping Brandon brainstorm the menu, anyway, and I loved that. It made sense for me to be in the kitchen with him. I remember thinking about it for days before I told him. I wondered if his jaw would fall off his face. Oddly, as I was writing this, I realized that I don't actually remember how he responded, so a couple of nights ago, I asked him.

"I was happy," he told me.

"That's all?" I said. "Not surprised? Not worried?"

"No." He smiled. "Just happy."

I would be the opening pantry cook, the *garde manger*.

I knew that wherever we went from here, the restaurant was opening, and I wanted to be standing inside of it when it did. If I wasn't there, I might never understand what it would ask of Brandon, or who he was becoming. Anyway, I was already inside, albeit unofficially: I had sneaked through the door in a hard hat, hiding from my uncertainty about writing, my career, everything I had thought I wanted. The restaurant had offered me a way out of a place that I was stuck in, and I took it. It did exactly what I hoped it would. It did it so well that it eventually brought me back to myself, and that was the trouble.

FRIED RICE WITH PORK AND KALE

Fried rice is one of my favorite things to eat, and it's also a convenient way to use up odd bits that collect in the fridge. We make it often for lunch, both on our ancient electric range at home and in the wood-burning oven at Delancey. The recipe below is intended to serve only as a guide, and you should run with it wherever you'd like, substituting as you go. Here are some tips to help you as you improvise.

- Instead of kale, try substituting chopped raw chard, sliced fennel bulb, chopped broccoli, snap peas, snow peas, chopped carrot, frozen peas (thawed, if possible), leftover roasted vegetables, or whatever you've got. In general, aim for at least one big handful of prepped vegetables per person. And if you're using frozen peas or leftover cooked vegetables, add them at the end, cooking them just long enough to warm through.
- We use smoked pulled pork in this recipe, but that's only because we often have it left over after eating at a barbecue restaurant in our neighborhood. You're welcome to try any other cooked meat instead: the slow-roasted

pork shoulder on page 291, or brisket, ribs, hot dogs, hot links, roasted chicken, Italian sausage, steak, cooked bacon, carnitas, pork tenderloin, and so on. Be sure to cut or tear the meat into bite-sized pieces. Or, if you want to use uncooked bacon, go for it: Four strips, chopped, is about right for this amount of rice, and you'll want to cook it first thing, starting with a cold, unoiled wok. If the bacon gives off a lot of fat as it cooks, pour a little off before proceeding, but reserve about a tablespoon for cooking the vegetables.

- Or, hey, try using shrimp. As with the bacon, you'll want to cook it first, before the vegetables. But in this case, get the wok nice and hot, and use some oil. When the shrimp is cooked, remove it from the wok while you cook the rest of the ingredients, and add it back at the end.

- If you happen to have some fresh ginger in the crisper drawer, try mincing a little and adding it early on, when you cook the vegetables. The same goes for sliced scallions. These aromatics are especially welcome if you're using a meat that's on the bland side, like roasted chicken or pork tenderloin.

- My favorite rice for frying is Calrose, but basmati and jasmine also work. Whatever you use, make sure it's thoroughly chilled before you begin, and it should ideally be a day old. We often pick up an extra to-go box of rice when we leave our favorite Korean or Chinese restaurants, or when we get Thai takeout.
- Chopped kimchi is wonderful in fried rice, especially with bacon and a little sesame oil.
- Few fried rices don't stand to benefit from the addition of some chopped fresh herbs at the end. I like cilantro and basil, and a little dill can be nice, too.
- I like to top my fried rice with an over-easy egg, cooked in a separate skillet. (Some people can decently fry eggs in a wok, but I am not one of them.) I also add a spoonful of hot sauce, such as *sambal oelek,* and a squeeze of lemon or lime.

1 bunch (about 250 g) kale, preferably lacinato
3 tablespoons peanut or grapeseed oil
Fine sea salt, to taste
2 teaspoons freshly squeezed lemon juice,

or to taste
4 cups (about 600 g) cold cooked rice
4 ounces (110 g) smoked pulled pork
1 tablespoon fish sauce, or more to taste
Unsalted butter (optional)

Wash and dry the kale leaves. Trim away and discard their woody stems, and then chop or tear the leaves into bite-sized pieces.

Heat a wok or large (12-inch) heavy skillet over high heat. When the pan is hot enough for a drop of water to instantly evaporate, add 1 tablespoon of the oil. Add the kale, and stir to coat. Cook, stirring occasionally, until the kale is wilted and beginning to char at the edges, 1 to 3 minutes. Add a good pinch of salt; then taste and adjust the seasoning as needed. Scrape the kale into a bowl, add 1 teaspoon of the lemon juice, and toss to mix.

With the wok still over high heat, add the rice, and then immediately add the remaining 2 tablespoons oil, drizzling it down the sides of the wok. Stir to coat the rice with oil. Then spread the rice all around the wok, so that as much of it touches the hot surface as possible, and let it cook, untouched, for 30 seconds to 1 minute, or until the rice on the bottom is browned and can be scraped away from the walls of the wok without resistance. Stir well, and then spread it out and let it sit again, untouched, for another 30 seconds to 1 minute. Continue to cook until the rice is evenly hot and browned to your liking. Then add the pork and 1 tablespoon fish sauce, stirring well. Continue to cook until the meat is heated through; then stir in the kale. Add the remaining 1 teaspoon lemon juice, and toss well. Taste for seasoning. If the rice is lacking salt, add more fish sauce, about 1/2 teaspoon at a time. If the flavor is a little flat, try adding 1 additional teaspoon of lemon juice. And if your meat is on the lean side or you find that the rice tastes dry, adding even 1/2 tablespoon of butter can work wonders.

Transfer the rice to a serving dish, taking care to scrape up any tasty browned bits that stick to the wok. Serve immediately.

Yield: 2 hearty servings

13

It was now July of 2009. We were nearly out of money. I had cleaned out my savings account to pay the rent and buy the point-of-sale computer system. But we were getting close. The construction was essentially done, or as done as it was going to get for the time being. Two members of our construction team (rhymes with "Holly" and "Landon") accidentally glued an eight-foot-tall chalkboard to the floor in the entryway and had to tease it up with razor blades, and the secondhand acoustic panels still needed to be screwed to the ceiling, the photographs and mirrors hung, and the computer system set up, but we were very close. And we seemed to remember how to cook, which felt promising, since that was the whole point.

Of course, before you can open a restaurant and legally sell food, you have to pass some inspections. This sounds supremely unexciting on paper, but in actuality, it's real edge-of-your-seat stuff, because each inspector tells you to do something that contradicts what the previous inspector told you to do. We had to repeat our plumbing inspection three times before passing, because one inspector insisted that we put a doll-sized floor sink on a pedestal underneath the stainless steel prep sink, a nonsensical demand that we nonetheless heeded, only to have the next inspector try to make us remove it. (For the record, it's still there, dutifully carrying out its purpose: to back up, overflow, and incite panic precisely at 5:01 p.m., as the host is seating the night's first customers.)

Then there's the building code inspection, which, when passed, gives you a very official-looking Certificate of Occupancy to hang on the wall. "Certificate of Occupancy," however, is no misnomer: it gave us permission to occupy the space, but not to actually *cook* anything. To do that, we'd have to pass the health inspection, the final obstacle standing between us and opening — aside, of course, from all the other details.

The first Sunday in July, we had a cleaning party. It was essentially a chain gang, but for public relations reasons, we decided that "party" was a better word. The place had been under construction for seven months, and it was still many layers of dust, dirt, and trash away from being a restaurant. There was no way that we could pass the health inspection without going after the room with a power-sprayer, or its human equivalent. So I sent out an e-mail to nearly every able-bodied person we knew in the city of Seattle, offering beer and greasy junk food in exchange for elbow grease.

I made a list of tasks, and as our kind, unsuspecting friends arrived, they claimed them. Tara scraped paint and old gummy tape from the front windows. Rebecca detailed the bathrooms. Mohini climbed to the top rung of a ladder and cleaned the pendant lights in the dining room and above the bar. Keaton brought an industrial vacuum from her husband Mark's metal shop and walked the perimeter with it. Ashley and Gabe sat on the sidewalk out front with a spray bottle of distilled vinegar and wads of steel wool, scrubbing rust from the shelves of a secondhand refrigerator. Myra scrubbed the inside of a secondhand reach-in fridge, and before she left, she took an *American Gothic*–style portrait of Brandon and me next to the front door, him with a pizza peel and me with a large spoon. It was hot out, and when evening finally came,

Brandon, Sam, and I opened a Belgian beer the size of a bottle of wine and sat out on the sidewalk, passing it back and forth.

The next morning, Brandon triumphantly called to request the health department inspection. The inspector assigned to our part of town curtly informed him that she was too busy to come. In fact, she would not be scheduling any inspections for a few weeks. After several minutes of begging, Brandon convinced her to give him the number of a guy assigned to a different part of town. This guy, as it turned out, was on vacation. But a couple of days later, he called back, and then, *boom,* we had a date for our final inspection. He would come the following day.

On the morning of the inspection, Ben met us at eight, wearing his denim overalls and old sneakers, to help tidy up the last corners and details. The three of us worked until noon, when the inspector's truck appeared at the curb outside. Ben sneaked out one door as the inspector walked in the other. I paced the bar and tried to look nonchalant while Brandon — who, by this point, was a certified expert in What Inspectors Want to Hear — showed the guy and his clipboard around. We passed. We could now open Delancey. The sun was out, so we got in the car, drove to Ben's (by this point, walking the half-block seemed too hard), and dragged him to a Mexican restaurant for celebratory midday margaritas.

The days that followed were a blur of pizza-testing, convection-oven buying, and kitchen-rearranging, and then, on Saturday evening, just as we were wrapping up a long day of errands, Brandon gashed his thumb on a sheet of steel in a home improvement store. I looked at his hand for an instant, just long enough to see a lot of blood, and then I opened my purse, took out a Kleenex, handed it to him, and privately began to hyperventilate.

Clearly, he was going to lose his thumb. He wouldn't be able to cook. Why hadn't we bought disability insurance? Why hadn't we had his hands insured for millions, the way pianists and hand models do? We were going to lose the restaurant before it was even open. We'd be up to our eyeballs in debt. With no restaurant, no job, and only one thumb, Brandon would fall in with a bad crowd. He wouldn't come home for weeks. I would cry myself to sleep. One night, high on desperation, he would commit a burglary, and he'd bring the stolen cash to me, promising to come home, to help me pay down our debt. *We'll start over,* he'd plead. But the cops would be after him, and we'd have to run. We'd go to Oklahoma City, to my mother's house. They'd never look for us there. He would live in the attic, and I would tell people that he was dead, and it would be awful, but we would still have each other.

We rushed to the emergency room. There was more bleeding. Four hours later, he was discharged with a hefty supply of gauze and medical tape and his thumb still intact. Which was useful, because later that week, we were finally going to use the kitchen at Delancey for something other than storing Doritos. We were going to host a private charity dinner, our first for paying guests.

For a couple of years, our Boat Street friend Olaiya had been running her own small catering company and in her spare time cooking charity dinners out of her house, sending the proceeds to help women survivors of war. Olaiya had been helping us with various Delancey-related tasks that spring and summer — setting up our accounts with produce vendors, researching aprons for the servers, making sure we were occasionally eating a proper meal — and at one of our meetings, she suggested that we do a charity dinner together at Delancey. It would be a low-pressure way for Brandon and me to get some practice before the official opening. So she rounded up twenty guests from her mailing list, and we were on.

It was a relief — a relief and a small terror — to actually cook again, instead of mixing concrete, moving equipment, or matching wits with inspectors. We were exhausted, but the adrenaline forced us on — and for me at least, so did the fear. I wanted the restaurant to succeed. I wanted people to like our food. I wanted someone to tell me that we weren't total idiots.

On the afternoon of the dinner, Olaiya set the tables with giant sunflowers. I went to the farmers' market and bought whatever looked good — bundles of small carrots, broccoli, bags of yellow potatoes, and a fat bunch of parsley — and we turned it into a wood oven–roasted starter. I cut the broccoli into florets and tossed them with olive oil, cumin, coriander, and salt, and when Brandon pulled them out of the oven, they were charred in spots and frizzled at the edges, so that they crunched softly, like water chestnuts, between your teeth. We drizzled them with a little lemon juice, and that was it. We left the carrots whole and roasted them quickly with olive oil and salt, so that they caramelized without turning to mush, and then they too got some lemon and a pinch of ground hot chile. And when the potatoes were crispy and browned, we sauced them with a parsley salsa verde. Olaiya's boyfriend poured wine, and Brandon made pizza after pizza after pizza, and then Olaiya and I scooped homemade vanilla malt ice cream into cups, until everyone was full. I stood at the dishwasher until 1 a.m., grinning like an idiot at the empty plates.

14

About three weeks out from our projected opening, we began hiring a staff. I guess it seems risky to wait so long, and it probably was, but it's not uncommon in the restaurant industry. You don't want to hire someone too far out, because unless you're a big corporate gig, you probably don't have a retainer to offer, and anyway, we were too busy with inspections and the last details of construction to think about anything but building codes and margaritas. Restaurants are works-in-progress even as they serve their first customers; that's why there are soft openings. You can train all you want, but a restaurant is unpredictable by nature: a refrigerator will break, or twenty-five customers will arrive at once, or a ten-person reservation will pull a no-show, or the table of drunks that you cut off will dump their water glasses on the floor in protest as they leave. (But if you're lucky,

183

one of the drunks will slink back an hour later, apologize to the host, and slip her a twenty.) The only way to work out the kinks is to smooth them as you go — and send a complimentary dessert to the next table over while you dash for the mop.

Neither of us had ever hired anyone. Because we lived in an apartment with a fairly upstanding landlord, we'd never even had to hire a plumber. We were always the ones being hired. We had always *been* employees (and sometimes, in my case, a mediocre one). Now we had to figure out how to be bosses, a tall order in any situation and an especially awkward one in ours, since we would likely be the same age as most of our staff. All we had going for us was gut instincts and Susan the Oracle.

We would likely need two servers and one host to run the dining room, which seats about forty people. The kitchen would need three cooks: a pizza cook to stretch the dough and put on the toppings, another cook to work the wood-burning oven, and a pantry cook to make starters and desserts. I would be the pantry cook, so that was taken care of, and Brandon has, from Day One, manned the oven. The baking of the pizzas is the trickiest part, he says, and like Domenico DeMarco of Di Fara, he wanted to do it himself. (That's why Delancey is open for dinner only, five nights a week; any more than that, and he'd burn out quickly and spectacularly, like a pizza left a minute too long in a 750° oven.)

We didn't have to put out a call for a host or servers. Our first host, Erin, lived in the neighborhood, heard about what we were doing, and stopped by one afternoon with a resume. She'd never worked in a restaurant, but she was articulate, well mannered, and pretty, a strawberry blonde with freckles across her nose. I also liked her outfit — a red-and-white polka-dotted blouse, I think. These were the kind of rigorous, painstaking criteria we used. She wanted to work five nights a week, and that was handy for us, because we wouldn't need to hire a second person for the job. If she was sick, maybe Olaiya could fill in, or Sam.

The first server we hired was Nicole, a friend of a friend of Olaiya's who had come to the charity dinner as a guest. She'd worked in a number of restaurants and was a natural server, able to simultaneously charm babies, key in an order on the fancy point-of-sale system, and tell Brandon a dirty joke. We hired her immediately. She brought in our second server, Tiffany, one of her coworkers from a previous restaurant.

Nicole wanted to work three days a week, and Tiffany wanted to work two. Few restaurant servers want to work what most people consider full-time. This is often because they're serving only to pay the bills, saving the rest of their time for doing the work they really want to do: writing, playing music, painting, acting, whathaveyou. Occasionally, and particularly at a busy restaurant, a server is able to make a lot of money with only a few shifts. In any case, we needed a third server in order to cover all the shifts each week. Toward the end of July, just as we were drafting an ad to post on Craigslist, an e-mail came in from a woman named Danielle. A longtime server and restaurant manager, she'd been reading my blog (at the suggestion of her friend David, who would also later work for us), had followed the progress of Delancey, and, on a whim, decided to send a resume. We brought her in for an interview and liked her from the start: she was warm and well spoken, with a broad smile and a tattoo of a tugboat on her forearm. She would wind up staying at Delancey for nearly four years — a decade in restaurant time, where employees generally come and go like cars through a tollbooth.

Finding a pizza cook was more complicated. Actually, to say that finding a pizza cook was more complicated is an understatement along the lines of *Michelle Obama has arms.* We posted an ad on Craigslist and expected two or three dozen replies, but this was smack-dab in the middle of the recession, so the responses totaled just under a hundred. Reading through them, we focused on two pieces of advice from Susan. First, there was the thing about hiring artists over trained cooks. It had worked well at Boat Street, but we had to ignore it: we didn't have time to teach someone to cook. Even after two years of testing his dough and practicing with a variety of ovens, Brandon was still only beginning to feel confident in his ability to make the kind of pizza he wanted to serve. We needed a cook who was already competent, who could contribute without requiring a lot of training. Of course, there's a balance to be struck, and Susan had mentioned that, too: we shouldn't hire someone who knew *too* much, who was overqualified for the position. For example, if you're looking for someone to stretch pizza dough, you probably shouldn't hire the guy who was the head chef of a fine dining restaurant for seven years. Nobody transitions easily from running his own kitchen to slinging dough for a couple of newbies. He would be bored stiff. He would probably try to take over the place, or, just as likely, quit within a month.

We whittled down the ninety-something applicants to four or five, and one by one, we brought them in for interviews. The most promising cover letter came from a cook named Jared. Actually, the fact that he had written a cover letter at all was promising; though we had specifically requested it in our ad, only a small number of people actually paid attention. "Serious Cook," read the subject line of his e-mail. *Magic words!* (Craigslist job seekers, NB: the subject "HIRE ME!!!!!" tends to produce a result opposite to the one intended.) Jared's first job had been as a pizza cook, he explained, and from there he went on to cook in kitchens around the country, mostly restaurants specializing in local, seasonal ingredients. *Nice!* He already had a job that filled his mornings, he confessed, but he wanted to do more. *A hard worker!* He even thanked us for our consideration. We were impressed.

The resume, however, was a problem. He had a BA and a culinary arts degree from one of the top schools. He had not only been a lead cook at two highly regarded restaurants in the Northwest, but he had cooked at the French Laundry — I recommend taking a moment here to let that sink in — *and* he had owned his own restaurant. Why would this guy now want to toss pizzas? He wouldn't even get to *cook*.

Despite these misgivings, we brought him in for an interview. Somehow, it seemed dumb not to. You never know. We wound up asking him about these crazy potato chips I'd seen in a magazine article about the French Laundry, potato chips with a sage leaf woven through each one. I can't explain what they're like without drawing a diagram; that's how complicated they are. Jared explained how he had made them. We did not offer him the job.

Instead, we offered it to a guy named John. He'd been stretching pizza for years. He looked to be a few years older than Brandon — in his early thirties, maybe — and he'd been stretching pizza since Brandon was in high school. He was tired of working for big restaurants that ran like machines, he said. He wanted a smaller place, one where he could feel like part of a family. The day after his interview, he and Brandon spent the afternoon making pizza together, trying it out. John made it look easy. He was perfect. He also, as Brandon learned, happened to write music for a hobby. They hit it off right away, shooting the breeze about instruments and editing software, the kind of things that people who write music shoot the breeze about. I remember feeling truly confident about Delancey after that day, feeling that we could safely open the doors now, that Delancey was actually going to be what Brandon had hoped it could be, because we had John on our team, and he knew pizza the way Jared knew sage-woven potato chips.

We asked him to come back for a second practice session about a week later, a Wednesday, the day before our first night of soft opening. My mom was in town to help with the last big push, and that Wednesday afternoon, she and I went to run errands. John was due to come in at three. I was having a few friends' photographs framed for Delancey's walls, so Mom and I went to pick them up, and then we went to Cash&Carry for some odds-and-ends supplies, and a little after four o'clock, we were at the grocery store, picking up baking powder and yeast and a bunch of sunflowers for the bar. I had just finished paying when my phone rang. It was Brandon. John didn't show up, he said. Brandon had tried calling him three times, and he hadn't answered. He'd also sent an e-mail, and in desperation, he'd gone to John's Myspace page (!) and left a note there.

I guess we could have kept hoping. We could have assumed that there had been some emergency, and that he would turn up shortly. I can't explain how we knew that he wasn't coming, not later, not anytime, but we did. It was July 29, which happened to be our second wedding anniversary, and we were due to open Delancey to its first paying guests, all of whom had made reservations weeks before, in approximately twenty-six hours.

I was reminiscing about John with Brandon last summer, if reminiscing is the appropriate word for an activity that makes you feel like driving a pencil through your eye. Even with the buffer of nearly four years, my throat tightened when we got to the phone call. I remember the disbelief most clearly. I couldn't believe that someone would *do that* to Brandon — this man who had quit school to go after the thing he most wanted, who had put his entire savings and ten months of physical labor into it, and now it was one day away from becoming a reality. I had had plenty of qualms about Delancey, and I had had plenty of quarrels with the man behind it, but even in my most Chicken Little hour, I had never thought of abandoning him. I had considered a number of possible outcomes, but leaving was not among them. I threw myself into the restaurant because I didn't want him, whether intentionally or not, to leave *me*. There were supposed to be three people in the kitchen at Delancey. Now we were down to two, and that's how we would open.

We were right about John: He never showed up. He didn't call or e-mail. We know he's alive, at least, because about a year later, a customer introduced himself to Brandon, saying that John had highly recommended the pizza at Delancey.

It was 103 degrees in Seattle on the day that John disappeared. The Pacific Northwest heat wave of July 2009 was so extreme that there's a Wikipedia entry for it. Like most buildings and homes in Seattle, the building Delancey is in has no air conditioning. Brandon made practice pizzas on his own for a couple of hours while my mom and I finished our errands. Then she took us out to dinner, for consolation and for our anniversary, and never before and never since has a cocktail been so necessary.

POPPY'S BOURBON SOUR

We went to dinner that night at a restaurant called Poppy, and this is the drink that I ordered. It's a classic, of course, and you might have a recipe for it already, but I think Poppy's version is particularly well balanced: bright, refreshing, and not too sweet. Jerry Traunfeld, the chef-owner, kindly agreed to put me in touch with Hideki Anpo, the restaurant's excellent bartender, and Hideki taught me how to make it.

A few quick tips:

- Don't worry about getting exactly three-quarters of an egg white. Just eyeball it, taking care to leave a little behind in the shell with the yolk.
- I recently saw a local grocery store selling tiny bottles of simple syrup for $7, and rather than responding as I wanted to (by smashing the entire display), I will just say this: There's no need, ever, to buy simple syrup. It's dead-easy to make. Poppy uses a 1:1 sugar-to-water ratio for theirs, and you can make it by combining 1 cup (200 g) granulated sugar and 1 cup (235 ml) boiling-hot water in a jar. Stir to dissolve the sugar, cool thoroughly, and it's ready to go. Store it in the refrigerator indefinitely.

- Lastly, Poppy serves their bourbon sour in a wine-tasting glass, but since few of us have those at home, I recommend a rocks glass.

3/4 egg white from a large egg
2 ounces (60 ml) Buffalo Trace bourbon, or whichever brand you prefer
1/2 ounce (15 ml) freshly squeezed lemon juice
1/4 ounce (7.5 ml) simple syrup
1 dash Angostura bitters
Ice cubes
A cherry or a slice of orange, for garnish (optional)

Combine the egg white, bourbon, lemon juice, simple syrup, and Angostura bitters in a shaker. Put on the lid — note that you're *not* adding ice at this point — and shake vigorously, counting to 13. Remove the lid, add a generous scoop of ice, put the lid back on, and shake again, counting to 13. Strain the drink into a glass, and add ice until the drink reaches the rim. Garnish, if you like, with a cherry or a slice of orange.

Yield: 1 serving

15

The next day, we cooked dinner for thirty people. Brandon, my mother, and I were in the kitchen. It was 96 degrees outside and, according to the laser thermometer gun that we bought for the wood oven, 105 degrees on the kitchen wall. The servers arrived in mid-afternoon to arrange the dining room into three long tables, and we propped open the doors while we worked. The ceiling fan was on high, spinning so violently that it blew out the candles as soon as they were lit.

My mother and I went to the farmers' market that afternoon and bought big beefsteak tomatoes, meaty green beans, fingerling potatoes, and farm eggs. For a first course, we made a composed salad, a bastard cousin of the Niçoise. We plated them on top of the reach-in refrigerator, the small prep table, the dish rack, any horizontal surface we could find — a game of

Twister with beans and potatoes and arms everywhere. We cut the tomatoes into thick slices and put a couple on each plate with a pile of blanched green beans on top and a spoonful of basil-shallot vinaigrette. Next to that went a fingerling potato with olive oil and crunchy salt, and next to that went half a boiled egg with olive oil and a single anchovy draped over the top. It was the kind of dead-simple salad I like to eat on a sweltering day, and our customers seemed to like it. Maybe they were just grateful that the ceiling fan was working and that the food wasn't hot.

Or maybe it's that our customers were mostly family, friends, and friends-of-friends. This was our very, very soft opening.

As new business owners go, we were lucky. I had a blog that was widely read, and my book had made the *New York Times* best-seller list. We were opening a pizza restaurant, and everyone, everyone loves pizza. We were getting a fair amount of press. On the one hand, this was thrilling. We were opening in a recession, but we had the immeasurable luxury of not worrying about whether people would come.

But the anticipation was also a problem. Brandon and I were trying something that we had never done before, and we were trying it *in public*. This wasn't like publishing a book. When you write a book, you get to workshop material with a small group of like-minded people, revise, work with an editor, revise again, work with a copyeditor, revise again, and then see two rounds of typeset proofs, all before the thing goes on sale. When you open a restaurant, people come in, eat your food, and if they don't like it, they tell everyone. There are few other pursuits in which you can have such a high-stakes debut. Just a month earlier, another highly anticipated restaurant had opened in our neighborhood, and on its first night, it was flooded with diners live-Tweeting their critiques and commentary. What we needed was to open quietly, to be allowed some time to learn how to run a restaurant. We had a lot of mistakes to make. We needed to protect ourselves somehow, possibly with body armor, to keep from being immediately trounced. That was our only chance of figuring out how to make good food at a reasonable speed, and to make our customers happy.

We owe Delancey's early success, and what small degree of sanity we still have, to our friend Ryan Bergsman. Most restaurants do two or three days of "soft opening," offering meals on an invitation-only basis to friends and family or just quietly unlocking the doors and seeing who shows up. But two or three days didn't feel like enough to us, and the let's-see-who-shows-up option sounded like strolling into the middle of the street and waiting to be hit by a car. Ryan and his wife, Kristen, had been helping us with construction, and he had an idea: that we should do an unusually long soft opening — seven nights in all — and make it reservation-only, strategically ramping up the number of reservations as the days went by. That way, we could incrementally work up to full capacity.

We would make July 30, a Thursday, our first night. Like our charity dinner with Olaiya, we would do a three-course fixed-price menu: twenty dollars per person, with beer and wine for three dollars a glass. We would serve only thirty people. We would take Friday and Saturday to regroup, and then we would do the same thing on Sunday. Then we would be open from Wednesday to Sunday of the following week, serving the full menu and taking first one and then two seatings of customers. (I should add that by this point in the process, we were out of cash, so we'd be buying each night's ingredients as we went, and slowly, we hoped, making some money to put toward our opening food-and-beverage inventory.) And the week after that, on Wednesday, August 12, 2009, we would open officially to the public.

That first Thursday began with Mom and me and the composed salads. Once they were plated and sent out, I went to the pizza station to help Brandon. We'd decided to do four types of pizza: Margherita, Brooklyn, Crimini, and Zucchini Anchovy. The pizzas at Delancey are about twelve inches across, and a very hungry person can put away a whole one on his own, but for the fixed-menu dinners, we served them family-style, so each person could taste a slice or two of each pizza. We would make six of each type, we figured, or maybe eight, until people cried uncle.

We started with the Margherita. Brandon would stretch the dough, lay it on the peel, and then I would put on the toppings. The sauce would go down first — a scant ladleful, or else the dough gets soggy. Then came the fresh mozzarella, which I tore into shreds as I went along. It takes approximately twenty seconds to hand-tear fifteen bite-size shreds from a ball of mozzarella and distribute them evenly across a pizza, but when it's over a hundred degrees in the room and there are thirty people waiting for you, it feels like twenty minutes. When I had finally finished, I nudged the peel toward Brandon, and then he rushed to slide the pizza into the oven, rushed to stretch a second, nudged it toward me, rotated the first, took the first out of the oven, and slid in the second, now topped and ready. Then he stretched a third and rotated the second while I sliced the first, drizzled it with olive oil, snipped a couple of fresh basil leaves over the top, and passed it to a server. Then I topped the third, and we went on like this — this, plus a lot of swearing — until we had made six. Then we moved on to the Brooklyn, which was like the Margherita, except before baking, it also got a handful of aged mozzarella, ground in a food processor to roughly the texture of potting soil, and afterward, it skipped the basil and olive oil in favor of a grating of Grana Padano. Then we made six of the Crimini, and then six of the Zucchini.

We made pizzas for probably an hour and a half, and then I went back to my station and, again with my mother, plated dessert: scoops of homemade vanilla malt ice cream in teacups, with a giant salted chocolate chip cookie wedged in the saucer. We hadn't been able to get a dishwasher for the night, so Brandon, Mom, and I were also taking turns doing the dishes. It was so hot back there, and so humid from the running of the dishwashing machine, that the ice cream began to melt the instant it landed in the cups. The servers grabbed them four at a time and nearly ran them to the dining room. One of the customers, the mother of a friend, stepped outside to cool off and fainted on the sidewalk.

The next morning, we slept in, and then we made a phone call to hire a new produce vendor, because the one we'd originally chosen (for year-round staples like crimini mushrooms, lemons, and fresh herbs) had messed up every single item in our first order. It's not complicated: the vendor had given us a weekly "fresh sheet," listing every item they offered and its brand or place of origin. But they delivered portabello mushrooms instead of crimini, conventional lemons from Mexico instead of organic lemons from California, and thyme not from a farm in central Washington but from someplace near San Diego.

Two days later, on Sunday morning, I drove my mother to the airport and cried the whole way home. I was on my own now. We were on our own. There would be no one to make sure that we remembered to

eat, no one to rub our backs, no one to re-
assure us, no soft parental buffer between
us and the very adult thing we were doing.
As she disappeared through the sliding
doors, I felt like screaming, *Waaaait! Don't
leave us alone with this thing!*

That night, we did our second dinner, also
a fixed menu. I wrote the courses on the
chalkboard that we'd accidentally glued to
the floor a couple of weeks earlier: farm
tomatoes, thickly sliced and topped with
corn cut straight from the cob, cherry
tomatoes, basil leaves, and basil-shallot
vinaigrette; four types of pizza; and then
more salted chocolate chip cookies, this
time served with blueberry yogurt popsicles
that I made in tall, narrow shot glasses. Our
friends Ashley and Gabe were there, and
Ashley later told me that they'd decided that
night to buy a house they'd been looking at
in the neighborhood, just so they would be
close to Delancey. This made us feel pretty
great, even if most real-estate experts would
not recommend choosing a house on the
basis of proximity to pizza. Ben was there
that night, too, and Brandon's old friend
Bonnie, who had been at our wedding.
Afterward, she sent us a thank-you note on
electric pink paper, telling us how proud
she was. I keep it pinned to the bulletin

board in my office, and I still get choked up when I read it.

We had somehow survived our debut as restaurant owners. The plan was working — or what was left of the plan, after a week-long heat wave and the disappearance of John. Now all we needed was a cook. The next morning, Brandon picked up the phone and called Jared. We didn't care what we had decided about him ten days earlier. We knew that he could do the job with his eyes closed, and we needed help.

He came right away. He still had another job that kept him busy until mid-afternoon, but he would get as many shifts covered as he could, and he would work for us three nights a week. To cover the other two nights, we hired another cook we'd decided against in the first go-round, a very nice guy who, as it turned out, was the slowest, sweatiest pizza stretcher the world has ever known. On our first official day, we opened to a line of customers that stretched down the block and around the corner. We were terrified. Brandon put on *Charlie Parker with Strings,* an album that had been my dad's, the most soothing music we had. Because any help is better than no help, we kept the slow guy for three weeks before Brandon gently let him go, our first official firing. Then our chef friend Danny came to the rescue, driving the hour-plus from Vashon Island, where he lives, to stretch pizza for us two nights a week. Every day was a new rescue operation, and it would be that way for a while.

TOMATO AND CORN SALAD WITH SHALLOT VINAIGRETTE

This is the salad that we served on our second night, and it stayed on the menu for weeks, until the end of tomato season. It's very, very simple, and there's no place to hide a mediocre tomato or starchy corn, so use the best you can get. It comes together quickly, but do note that the vinaigrette should be started ahead of time — at least an hour and a half before you plan to eat, or even earlier — so that the shallots and garlic have time to be lightly pickled by the vinegar.

At home, we like to eat this salad with buttery scrambled eggs, some chewy bread, and a wedge of extra-sharp cheddar cheese. And I highly recommend this: When the platter of salad is nearly empty, take a crusty hunk of bread, sop up the last shallots and tomato juices with it, balance a sliver of cheddar on top, and eat.

For the Vinaigrette
2 small or 1 medium shallot (about 50 g), minced
1 medium clove garlic, minced
5 tablespoons (70 ml) red wine vinegar
1/2 cup (120 ml) olive oil
1/8 teaspoon sugar

A good pinch of fine sea salt, or more to
  taste
4 or 5 fresh basil leaves

For the Salad
2 large beefsteak tomatoes, or 6 smaller
  tomatoes
1 or 2 handfuls of cherry tomatoes
Raw kernels from 1 ear of corn
Crunchy salt, such as Maldon or fleur de
  sel
A few fresh basil leaves

Make the Vinaigrette
Stir together the shallots, garlic, and vinegar
in a small bowl. Set aside for 1 hour — or
even a couple of hours, if you have time.
You're looking to soften the flavors of the
shallot and garlic, so that they no longer
taste raw; they should taste lightly pickled.

Whisk in the olive oil, sugar, and salt. Add
the basil leaves, bashing them with the
whisk to bruise them and release their oils.
Let sit for another 30 minutes. Before using, remove and discard the basil leaves,
and taste for salt.

Assemble the Salad
Slice the tomatoes into 1/2-inch-thick
rounds. Arrange them on a platter. Halve

the cherry tomatoes, and strew them around the tomato slices. Scatter the raw corn kernels on top. Season with a good pinch of crunchy salt. Spoon the vinaigrette liberally over the whole platter — 1/4 cup wouldn't be too much; you'll want extra for eating with bread — and then snip the basil leaves into strips over the top.

NOTE: Leftover vinaigrette can be covered and stored in the refrigerator for up to 3 days. (After that point, the flavor of the garlic and shallot can get too strong.) Bring to room temperature before using.

Yield: 4 to 6 servings

16

In the beginning, we were both at the restaurant seventeen hours a day. Maybe only fifteen, if we were lucky. We couldn't afford a prep cook, so we did everything ourselves.

We'd get there at nine, because the deliveries begin arriving then, and if you're not there to unlock the door, you don't get your delivery. The single guys who've worked at Delancey would probably also like me to note that if you're not there, you don't get to see that pretty olive-skinned girl from Billy Allstot's farm bend over in her tight jeans, hoisting cases of fresh tomatoes out of a truck spray-painted with a mural of vegetables. She delivers at nine on the dot. Prep cooks start the day early, and restaurant vendors start even earlier.

But at Delancey, the pizza dough is more important than any delivery. It has to be checked first thing in the morning, to monitor its rise. The dough for any given day is made the previous day, and in general, the slower the rise, the more flavor you'll taste in the pizza. As of this writing, almost four years into running Delancey, the dough is made around 11:30 a.m. in the winter and 2:30 p.m. in the summer, and it's ready around 11:30 the following morning. We use very little yeast so that even on a hot day, when the yeast is more active than on cooler days, the dough still rises slowly over eighteen to twenty-four hours. I will never understand why pizza is considered a fast food.

But when we opened, everything was trial and error. From day to day, our greatest fear was that the dough wouldn't rise in time — or, worse, wouldn't rise at all, which would mean that we had nothing to sell. We needed each day's dough to be risen and ready within a narrow window of time, between 9 a.m. and 1 p.m. Any earlier, and we wouldn't be there; any later, and there wouldn't be time to portion it and then shape the portions into balls. That was one issue.

The second was that, although Brandon had been testing and retesting the dough for more than a year, he had never made it on a day when the temperature went above

86°F, because temperatures above 86°F are hard to come by in Seattle. But of course, there we were in a heat wave. So between the 750°F pizza oven, a convection oven, and the industrial dishwasher that runs almost constantly from 4:30 p.m. to 11:30 p.m., all within about 250 square feet, the kitchen was rarely below 90°F for weeks. We were back there sweating our brains out, steam-room-style, and all we could think about was how to keep the dough from rising too fast. An easy solution, of course, would have been to use less yeast, but we already weren't using much — about a teaspoon for every seven pounds of flour, for the baking nerds out there. We were afraid to use any less (though we now know that we can, and in hot weather, we do). If we had had a nice, roomy walk-in refrigerator, we wouldn't have had to worry: We could have used as much yeast as we wanted and made the dough at any time of day. We could have shoved it in the fridge to slow the rise as needed. But we didn't have a walk-in.

For the first months, we made the dough at the end of the night, after service. It took about nine to twelve hours to rise — much less than the eighteen hours Brandon was aiming for — and if we made the dough at midnight, the timing was just right. In other words, the dough got more sleep than we did. Our thirty-quart mixer can hold enough dough to yield about forty pizzas, and we would make three batches each night. Once each was mixed, Brandon would give it a final stir with a giant wooden spoon and then scrape it into a tub. We would snap lids on the tubs and then leave them to rest overnight in one of several places, depending on the ambient temperature of the kitchen. If the temperature was moderate, we would leave them on top of the pizza station, facing the closed mouth of the oven. If it was a little warmer, we would leave them on the shelves next to the pizza station, a little farther from the mouth. If it was actually hot, they would go on the shelf underneath the pizza station, just a few inches from the ground. If it was even hotter than that, we would carry them into the dining room, where it's always fairly cool, and leave them on a table. When it was historic-heat-wave-hot, we heaved the tubs into the back of our car, drove them to our apartment, huff-and-puffed them down the stairs to the basement, the only place left in town where a person could comfortably wear long sleeves, and stored them there until morning, when we reversed our steps.

Wherever it was, the dough had to be checked first thing. Through trial and error, Brandon figured out the optimal rise level, and he marked it with a Sharpie on the outside of each dough tub. If the dough was over the line by 9 a.m., the rise was too fast and the flavor could be diminished. There was a lot of swearing. Ideally, it would still be a little below the line and could be left to continue rising naturally for another hour or two. If it was *way* too low, Brandon would put the tubs somewhere warm — usually on top of a refrigerator — to speed the rise.

There's still an element of precariousness to the process, even after doing it close to a thousand times. But at the start, every day was pure touch-and-go.

So, before we had a prep cook, Brandon and I would rush to the restaurant at 9 a.m. He would check on the dough. Then there would be deliveries to receive and put away. Around 11:00, the oven would need to be lit. The night before, at closing, he or the pizza cook would have leaned a small steel door over the mouth of the oven, and the next morning, when the door was lifted away, the oven temperature would still be about 400°F. Brandon would sweep out the old ash and then build a fire — roughly the same size as one you'd build in your home fireplace — on top of the previous night's still-glowing coals. Within a couple of hours, the oven would be hot enough that any soot on its ceiling would have burned clean away, and this meant that the oven was at least 700°F, an important marker. From this point, it would take about three hours for the oven to be ready for cooking, heated properly from edge to edge. Of course, Brandon would want me to clarify that the oven isn't one single temperature from edge to edge, and that's part of what's so great (and exhausting) about cooking in it: it's about 400°F near the mouth and close to 1,000°F way up in the dome. To get each pizza exactly the way he wants it, he obsessively rotates, wiggles, lifts, and otherwise repositions it an average of ten times in its approximately three and a half minutes in the oven.

Anyway, while the oven heated, there would inevitably be a piece of equipment to fix. Because we had bought almost all of our equipment used, most of it broke within the first year. One morning, it might be the bar fridge, which needed a new compressor after about a week of use and finally got one after four months. Another day, the problem might be the small fridge that we used for storing the dough once it had been portioned into balls. It refused to get any colder than 55°F, and it needed constant tweaking to achieve even that. On our first day of soft opening, three hours before the guests arrived, the mirror in the empty bathroom spontaneously fell off the wall, slamming onto the sink and somehow managing to turn on the faucet before hitting the floor, where it shattered triumphantly. Not long after, the toilet paper dispenser shimmied loose from the wall, leaving behind a quarter-sized hole. We had bought a residential-grade dispenser rather than a commercial one, failing to note that most residences don't have a hundred-plus people using the toilet each day.

When whatever had broken was fixed, or when a repairman was assuredly on his way, Brandon would start prepping the pizza station. He would drain the tomatoes for sauce, grind the Grana in the food processor, slice mushrooms on the mandoline. That went on for a while, and then, around lunchtime, he would start portioning the three tubs of dough into 126 pizza-sized lumps and hand-shaping those lumps into 126 balls. In the beginning, it would take him three hours to weigh and shape them all. While he worked, he would prop his laptop on the shelf above his station and stream B-movies or second-string cable TV shows. *Prison Break,* he reported, is remarkably transporting when you're a prisoner of dough.

To be honest, I don't know what I did all morning. But somehow, it would suddenly be lunchtime. I think I spent a lot of time cleaning. I was always cleaning something, because *everything* gets dirty in a restaurant. You wouldn't believe how many people manage not only to spill their wine, but to spill it onto a wall. We didn't know that when we chose a flat white paint for Delancey's dining room. I can now tell you that red wine, hastily wiped up and left overnight, leaves a stain that looks a lot like a fresh bruise.

I was also very busy obsessing over the glasses. There's no reason to think about this unless you've worked in a restaurant, but every glass — wine, water, beer, or otherwise — that comes out of the dishwasher needs to be dried and polished by hand before being put on the shelf and used again. And you can't polish them with just anything, because you don't want to leave lint behind. You need to use a microfiber cloth, or a clean cloth napkin with a tight weave. And you have to wash your hands before you begin, even if your hands are *technically* clean, because you probably have just enough oil on them to leave finger-prints. And don't forget to hold the glass up to the light as you're wiping it, to check for smudges and residue and lint. On a busy night, nobody had time to exorcise their obsessive-compulsive disorder on the glasses, so sometimes, while Brandon tended to the dough, I would rewash and redry every glass in the restaurant.

Then I would prep my station, running down a list of all the ingredients that I would need and washing, chopping, or otherwise preparing as much of them as I expected to use that evening. When we first opened, this would take all afternoon, even though I was responsible for only two or three salads and two desserts. I was a very slow prepper. I didn't know how to work any faster. The truly tragic part is that my slowness created a vicious cycle: because I was slow, I could never prep quite enough, so by mid-service, I would run out of some ingredient and have to rush to prep more between orders. If the ingredient in question was cherry tomatoes, it was no big deal: they just had to be plopped into a strainer and held under the tap. But I was up a creek if it was foraged wild watercress, which cannot be prepped at any speed faster than plodding, lest you fail to notice a crumb-sized snail or worm or other streambed cargo on the underside of a leaf and only learn of it when the diner sends the entire salad back to the kitchen in disgust.

In any case, once we were prepped and ready, or poorly prepped and somewhat ready, we'd serve our customers. We'd do that from 5 p.m. until the last table was seated around 10, which meant that we were finished cooking around 10:30 or 11. While we waited for the last customers to leave, Brandon might lie down and nap on the sacks of flour on the shelf under his station. Then we'd clean up, which meant packing up our leftover ingredients, wiping down and sanitizing the stations, and then sweeping and mopping. Sadistic dictators should equip their labor camps with pizzerias instead of cafeterias, because sweeping and mopping the room where a person has been tossing flour-dusted pizza dough for five hours is the purest form of punishment I know.

Finally, around midnight, we would start making the next day's dough. This required musical accompaniment, or else we would fall asleep. Most nights, we would put on an album by the band Elvis Perkins in Dearland and turn it up loud. (The opening song began, "Sweep up, little sweeper boy, sweep up." I felt a real affinity with that boy.) I would weigh out the yeast, salt, water, and flour while Brandon operated the mixer, and when one batch was done, we would do it again a second time, and then a third time. Then I would sweep some more, because there would be a whole new layer of stuff on the floor.

When I would tell people about what our days were like then, they would often say that it sounded a lot like having a newborn baby. Not having had one, I only sort of knew what they meant, but I remember being comforted by the idea anyway, by the sense that other people understood — and even more, by the knowledge that, even when everything went wrong, at least the restaurant, and the dough, always slept through the night.

STONE FRUIT WITH PROSCIUTTO AND MOZZARELLA

That summer and fall at Delancey, between prep work and other tasks, Brandon and I would often build a quick cold lunch around whatever we found in the refrigerators: one stray plum, let's say, or the last handful of arugula, or a sample of salami sent by one of our vendors. My favorite of these lunches — and one I've repeated many times since — was a composed salad assembled from a cold, perfect nectarine, the last of a leg of prosciutto, a hunk of fresh mozzarella, and plenty of our best olive oil. You could make a similar dish with any stone fruit or melon, of course, and with any kind of cured ham, but what follows is my loose version. Feel free to use more or less of any ingredient, depending on what you've got.

1 ripe nectarine, pitted
1 ball of fresh mozzarella
6 to 8 thin slices of prosciutto
A small handful of fresh parsley, mint, or
  basil leaves (optional)
A fistful of arugula (optional)
A squeeze of fresh lemon juice (optional)
Olive oil

Crunchy salt, such as Maldon or fleur de
  sel
Bread

Slice the nectarine thin, so you wind up
with about a dozen slices. Divide the slices
between two plates. (Or, if two plates
sounds like a lot of work, use one small platter and share it. That's what we did.) Tear
the mozzarella into bite-sized nubs, and
scatter them over the slices of nectarine.
Tear the prosciutto into bite-sized pieces,
and drape them over the top. If you'd like,
scatter some fresh herbs or arugula around
the plate, too, and maybe squeeze a little
lemon juice over them. Finally, give each
plate a generous drizzle of olive oil, and salt
to taste. Serve with plenty of bread for mopping up the juices.

Yield: 2 servings

17

It is a very nice thing to be your own boss, presuming that you know how to do your job. But I knew almost nothing about co-owning a restaurant, and only a little more than that about cooking in one.

I was a slow prepper, and I was a slow pantry cook. My job was to plate cold dishes, which meant salads and most desserts. Pantry cooks are sometimes also in charge of hot dishes that can be quickly rewarmed and plated, with little actual cooking involved. The station requires organization and precision, like every station in a professional kitchen, but it's not considered difficult. In most restaurants, pantry cook — or *garde manger* in the classic French kitchen — is an entry-level position, one that does not come with a lot of cachet or require the ability to tell if a steak is medium rare just by looking at it. When (or, rather, *if ever*) you find a pantry cook on a reality TV show about restaurants, he or she will not be presented as a tattooed badass with a hot girlfriend.

I understood all of that. I'd worked the pantry station during my restaurant internship in college, though that had been ten years earlier. Also, the internship was only eight weeks long, and the other cooks had made it exceptionally easy. Cakes, compotes, ice creams, and anything else on the dessert menu was prepared by the pastry chef: all I had to do was slice or scoop. If I was to plate a hot dish — a chickpea stew, let's say — it would be waiting in a chafing dish when I arrived. If I needed to slice kumquats for a salad, someone would tell me exactly how much to prep. I didn't have to guess, and I never ran out mid-service. I figured the other cooks were just being nice, trying to ease me in gently. Now I get it: they were trying to save themselves some trouble. Any mistakes the newbie made would probably fall to them to fix, so they might as well babysit her from the outset.

In order to run my station at Delancey, I had to first buy enough of each ingredient to serve a given night's diners. I've made plenty of grocery lists, but scaling up to restaurant dimensions struck me as nearly impossible to do without consulting a psychic. There's no way to know how many diners will come in or how many of each menu item they will order. One way to handle the situation would be to buy a lot of everything, Costco-style. But a restaurant is trying to make a profit, and a home cook is not. Food waste in a home kitchen is lamentable, but food waste in a restaurant kitchen can be fatal. Also, because we didn't have a walk-in, refrigerator space was tight. (Actually, space in general was tight. While fresh tomatoes and peppers were in season, we stored cases of them under a bookshelf by the front door because there was no room in the kitchen.) The fact that I ever figured out how to buy for my station is due entirely to our friend Olaiya, who looked over our menus for the soft opening and walked me through a calculation of each ingredient quantity, stopping just short of holding my hand. Once I had made it through the soft opening, I had a decent idea of what I would need each night. Of course, that didn't mean that I would be able to get it washed, chopped, and other-wise prepped before the doors opened. I never really mastered that part.

I also knew very little about the flow of a restaurant kitchen during service. When a server takes a table's order, that information has to be transferred somehow to the kitchen, and to the relevant cook. Telepathy would be fastest, but most restaurants use point-of-sale computer systems. The server taps in her orders on a screen at the edge of the dining room, and the orders show up, a second later, on tickets that spit from a small printer in the kitchen. It's a tidy system, but it has its problems: namely, no one ever has to talk to, or even look at, anyone else. When an order gets messed up, it's easy for the staff to split along team lines, the front of the house versus the back of the house.

This tendency is rooted, I think, in industry-wide discrepancies between what cooks earn and what servers earn. Cooks work longer hours than servers, but almost without exception, they make less money. Many states have tried to alleviate the problem by creating a lower minimum wage for tipped employees like servers, but that helps only so much, because tips can still tip (*har har*) the balance. And then there are states like Washington, where the minimum wage is the same across the board — and, as of this writing, the highest in the country. Brandon and I have taken our own steps to try to equalize pay at Delancey, giving our cooks above-average wages plus a share of the nightly tips, but a server at Delancey can still wind up taking home more than a cook.

In any case, we wanted to use a computerized order system. It simplifies accounting and a whole bunch of other tasks that we're bad at. But we also wanted to cultivate a pleasant working environment. We didn't want our staff to wind up treating each other, or us, like rivals in a National Hockey League game.

About a month before the soft opening, we ran into Renee, one of the owners of Boat Street, and when I mentioned my uncertainties about working in the kitchen at Delancey, she invited me to observe her kitchen at Boat Street one night. I arrived around two in the afternoon and, trying to be useful, busied myself with pitting a giant bag of Montmorency sour cherries from a tree in Renee's yard (!) while I watched the cooks set up for the evening. When the diners began to arrive, I noticed something: there was no printer in the kitchen. The printer was in the dining room, next to the computer terminal, a good fifteen or twenty paces from the kitchen. Each time a server entered a new order, she had to grab the ticket herself, walk the ticket all the way back to the kitchen, announce it to the relevant cook, and lay it down on a designated table. It was inconvenient for the servers, but conveniently, it meant that they spent a lot of time with the cooks — dropping off, picking up, checking in, and, inevitably, chatting. That was when I figured out why Boat Street feels the way it does: like any good dinner party, everybody winds up hanging out in the kitchen.

So we bought only one printer for Delancey, and it sits next to the bar. It's not an ideal setup; when a server has an order for the pantry station, she must carefully escort it past the wood-burning oven, risking an accidental jabbing from the long handle of Brandon's peel as he retrieves a pizza. At the outset, we weren't sure whether it would be the secret to our success or an instant worker's compensation lawsuit. But I am pleased, if somewhat surprised, to report that no one has been injured. Whether by luck or by design, the system works, and the cooks and servers not only talk to one another but actually seem to like one another.

In mid-September, we decided that we could afford to hire a prep cook. Jared quit his other job and came to work for us full-time, picking up three morning prep shifts in addition to his three nights. This meant that, most mornings, Brandon could now go in around eleven, and I could go in sometime between noon and two, depending on the day's prep list. We would still get home very late, but we were getting more sleep. It also helped that now we knew what to expect. In the beginning, I would be mopping the kitchen floor after the last customer had gone home, thinking, *I can't believe I have to mop this stupid, stupid, stupid floor. Why does pizza have to be so messy? Why is pizza so STUPID? Maybe if I impale myself on this broom handle, I can go to the hospital, and MAYBE THERE I CAN ACTUALLY GET SOME SLEEP.* But after we had a prep cook, and after a few weeks had gone by, I began to think, *Right. Here I am again, mopping the floor at one in the morning. This is what I do now.* The restaurant was dependent on us, and it wasn't going to stop depending on us. But we could begin to adjust, and we could begin to find ways, like hiring Jared to work more shifts, to make it adjust to us.

And it wasn't like Delancey was a constant grind. There was more to it than that. It was the hardest work I had ever done, physically and otherwise, but sometimes I'd be standing at my station, absorbed in a task, when I'd suddenly think, *I KNEW IT! I wasn't supposed to be a writer! I'm supposed to be a cook! I'm supposed to help run this restaurant! Ding ding ding!*

I was learning. We were learning. I asked Susan the Oracle about her bookkeeping system at Boat Street, and she invited me in to watch her process a day's receipts. Sitting next to her in the cramped back office, hunched over spreadsheets and files, I was so overwhelmed that I cried. Susan and I are not the kind of friends who comfortably get weepy together, but she patted my shoulder. Back at Delancey, Brandon and I sat down and hashed out our own system. Together we worked out tip-sharing percentages for the staff, and then I taught myself how to do payroll. Only the first three times did I come close to screaming. I now do payroll every other Monday, using my TI-85 graphing calculator from high school trigonometry. I get to make charts and fill in boxes and make neat bundles of receipts and nightly tallies. Like fetishes and pet names, this kind of loaded information is perhaps best reserved for intimates, but I really, really like doing payroll.

And once the initial panic wore off, there was a lot to like about professional cooking. I might never have survived as a pantry cook in another chef's kitchen, but at Delancey, there was no one to report to except myself and Brandon and our customers. The food we were serving was the kind of stuff that we wanted to eat ourselves, the kind we like to make at home. We were using great ingredients, keeping it straightforward, trying to make every bite as good as possible. Why make things complicated when it's hard enough to do simple things well? I've never been drawn to restaurants where every menu item has a dozen different flavors going on, the kind of place that serves a dish like Grilled Entrecote Steak and Charred Red Onions with Caramelized Turnips, Tarragon-Spinach-Potato-Cheddar Gratin, and Cabernet Grape Reduction (an actual dish I saw on a menu recently). When we opened, our menu had two starters: a salad of spiky wild arugula from the farmers' market, with radishes, shaved Grana Padano, and a Champagne vinaigrette; and the sliced tomato salad from our soft opening, with kernels of sweet corn, basil leaves, and shallot vinaigrette. After that, there were eight pizzas, and then three desserts: a chocolate chip cookie, a raspberry popsicle in a shot glass, and sliced peaches in white wine.

Brandon's job was, of course, to obsess

over the middle portion of the menu, the pizza. My job was to obsess over everything else. Obsession is a job I know how to do. Each tomato salad started with a whole, sliced beefsteak tomato, and because there would be no way to fix it if the tomato was insipid or mealy, I tasted a sliver from each one as I sliced it. I probably ate the equivalent of a tomato a night, meted out in quarter-sized portions. When an order for a popsicle would come in, I'd pull it out of the freezer and dip it cautiously into a tub of warm water, like a reluctant swimmer, until it was defrosted *just* enough that the diner could twist the stick and ease the popsicle out of its holder. When the arugula started to wane and we switched to butter lettuce with a red wine vinaigrette, I found that I loved, and I mean *loved,* plating it: making sure each square centimeter of each lettuce leaf was lightly and evenly coated in dressing and then stacking them, largest leaf on the bottom to smallest leaf on top, like a child's nesting blocks. Nothing about my life looked the way it had a few months earlier, but I could make a salad that looked really, really nice.

For the first two or three months, there was no sign outside the restaurant, because we hadn't gotten around to having Sam, who is a designer, do a logo. But we talked about it a lot, the same way we talked about making a stamp of the logo and stamping the top of each menu in orange-red ink, to match the paint color of the pendant lights in the dining room. But until we had that logo, I wrote *delancey* by hand on every menu every night. I was usually getting to the task around 4:59 p.m., as the line of customers began to fidget out front, and each time I would finish a half-dozen or so menus, one of the servers would run them to the host, so that she could hand them out as she seated the tables. Sometimes my mind would wander midway through the stack and I'd lose my ability to spell. But I liked it, and Brandon did, too — the idea that, like pretty much everything in the place, we were even making the menus by hand. When we did finally get around to doing some signage, we decided to scrap the logo plan and just use my handwriting, blown up and painted on the front window. We still have no stamp, though I'm working on it.

There were many moments early on when I wondered if it wouldn't be better to be eaten alive by a wild animal than to show up for work. But in the midst of those hours, there was one that I always loved. It begins around 3:30 p.m., when the servers set up the dining room. They set the tables, light the votives, and fill the water glasses. On the surface, it seems pretty mundane. Sometimes it also includes a bit of chaos, like when a wine delivery has come late and there are enough cardboard boxes in the entryway that passersby, on more than one occasion, have asked if we're moving or going out of business. But even then, for that hour, the room has this calm, consistent thrum to it, a sort of potential energy that feels peaceful and reassuring. I looked forward to it every day, and I still do.

CHILLED PEACHES IN WINE

This was one of our opening desserts, and the recipe is based on an idea I found in David Tanis's first cookbook, *A Platter of Figs*. For the wine, you don't need anything expensive: just a light, crisp, dry white. You can also try this method with a rosé of similar character. And for the peaches, it doesn't matter whether they're white or yellow: just be sure to use great, fragrant ones with firm, dense flesh. This recipe depends almost entirely on the quality of the fruit. (At Delancey that summer, we used peaches from Frog Hollow Farm in California, growers of the best stone fruits I've had.) You can serve them after only a few hours in the wine, but after twelve hours — or twenty-four, if you're good at advance planning — they're translucent, totally boozy, and very much worth the wait.

This recipe is also wonderful with nectarines.

4 medium-sized ripe peaches (700 g, or about 1 1/2 pounds), rinsed and patted dry

2 tablespoons (25 g) sugar, or more to taste

2 cups (475 ml) crisp, dry white wine or rosé

Slice the peaches very thin (I aim to get 12 to 16 slices per peach). Combine the peaches and sugar in a large bowl or storage container, and toss gently to mix. Add the wine, and toss gently again. Taste, and if you'd like more sweetness, add sugar, a tablespoon at a time. Brandon likes these peaches a little sweeter than I do, so for him, I might use 4 tablespoons in all. When they're sweetened to your liking, cover the container and refrigerate for several hours — or up to a day.

Serve the peaches very cold, straight from the refrigerator, in short, wide glasses, with a small ladleful of their liquid. Eat the peaches, and then drink the liquid left in the glass.

Yield: 4 to 6 servings

A TRICK FOR RED WINE VINAIGRETTE

Brandon loves to make vinegar, and one of the first salads we served at Delancey had a mustardy vinaigrette that used his home-made red wine vinegar. But after only a couple of weeks, we ran out of our stash. The vinegars that we could buy on short notice seemed thin and tinny in comparison, so Brandon devised this trick. It turns out that if you add even a little bit of red wine (ideally a fruity, light- to medium-bodied, not-too-tannic type) to your red wine vinaigrette, you can boost and deepen the flavor of the dressing, making up for imperfections in your vinegar. It makes a grocery store vinegar taste like a fancy one.

A word about Dijon mustard: We like our vinaigrettes on the mustardy side, and over the course of a lot of salads, we've discovered a few things about brands of mustard. Grey Poupon, it turns out, can taste bitter in large quantities, and Maille can taste too salty. Instead, keep an eye out for Roland Extra Strong, Beaufor, or Edmond Fallot. We use them interchangeably. They're not too expensive, pretty easy to find — two of them are sold at our neighborhood grocery store — and their flavor is balanced but insistent. We use them for everything.

I like this dressing best on tender lettuces, with thinly sliced fennel or radishes and shavings of Parmigiano-Reggiano. But it'll be delicious on anything you've got.

2 tablespoons Dijon mustard
1 1/2 tablespoons red wine vinegar
2 teaspoons red wine
Pinch of fine sea salt
Pinch of sugar
1/4 cup (60 ml) olive oil

In a jar or small bowl, whisk together the mustard, vinegar, wine, salt, and sugar. Gradually add the olive oil, whisking to emulsify. The dressing should look opaque and somewhat creamy, almost peachy in color.

NOTE: This dressing will keep in the refrigerator indefinitely.

Yield: about 1/2 cup

18

Jared was our first full-time employee. He was the first person to throw himself in as far and as deep as we had. He was excited about the place, and he had copious energy to put into it. He wanted the same thing we wanted: for the restaurant to not only succeed, but also to be a very good place to eat. He had some cheffy tendencies that weren't our taste, like wanting the salads to be taller and more elaborate, and he was desperate to put a *boca negra* on the dessert menu, a "chocolate decadence"–style cake he used to serve at his own restaurant. But he did things the way we asked him to, and often better than we could.

But let's get to the important part: Jared was *ripped*. Most nights, he wore a turquoise do-rag, so he looked like he was ready to dead lift at Muscle Beach. He was also handsome. You would think the do-rag would cancel out that fact, but miraculously, it didn't. He looked a little like Axl Rose circa 1991, the *Use Your Illusion* era. When I first came to that realization, I felt compelled to watch the "November Rain" video over and over on YouTube for half an hour, so if you need to put the book down and do the same, I get it. Don't miss the kiss that Axl gives Stephanie Seymour at their "wedding." When I was thirteen, it was the sexiest thing I'd ever seen.

Jared wore cologne, possibly Drakkar Noir. He called me "Molls," which seemed weird, but I was touched that he felt comfortable enough to give me a nickname. In fact, he felt comfortable enough to, on occasion, plant himself in front of my station and strike up a chat while he changed his shirt at the end of the night. I would go rigid as a piece of furniture and fix my eyes on the plate in front of me, hoping that my silent concentration said, *Hey, no biggie! No biggie at all! Ha ha ha! Nothing inappropriate happening here, HAAAAAA HA! Just plating this apple crisp!*

When he came to work for us, he had a girlfriend who would often come in for dinner. She was pretty in a Carmen Electra way, and she had outstanding cleavage. When she left, he would walk her to the door and stand there, where we could all

239

see them, while he wrapped his arms around her waist and pressed himself against her, smiling the way you might smile at someone you're in the process of undressing. During lulls in service, he sometimes did push-ups on the floor in front of the convection oven.

Jared didn't drink. We noticed right away that he didn't want to taste the samples that our wine reps brought around, and we assumed that we should stop offering. We didn't know his story, but the first hint came only a few weeks after we hired him, when one of his former bosses came in for dinner and asked the server how Jared was doing.

"Oh, he's great! Doing really well," she said.

"You mean he's not drinking?" the guy asked.

It's not the kind of comment that you can ordinarily brush aside, but Jared was sober, and what he had been before was not ours to ask. Eventually, maybe because we were tired or working a lot, or because we needed him, or maybe a combination of all three, we forgot that the conversation had happened at all.

About two months in, sometime in October, Jared started pouring himself half a beer at the end of the night. Shortly after that, he started pouring himself a whole pint. One morning, Brandon saw him help himself to a beer at the end of his prep shift. But Jared wasn't working that night, and it had been a hectic morning, the kind that could cause anyone to want a midday drink, so Brandon didn't think much about it. In any case, Jared seemed to know exactly how far he could go without stretching the limits of our gullibility. We wouldn't know the full extent of his issues for several more weeks, until other staff members told us that his midday beers were not an unusual occurrence and that he'd been bullying them into doing work that was his to do.

I catch myself pausing when I write about Jared, because I want to believe that he's sober again. Sometimes I wonder if he will read this book. I don't think he's a bad person. In spite of his ego and his exhibitionism, he was someone we thought of as a friend. Brandon once bought him a powder-blue electric bass guitar, just because he saw it at a thrift shop and knew that Jared would like it. For the first couple of months, we couldn't have run Delancey without him. The trouble was that Jared knew it, and even when it was no longer the case, he still believed it.

Brandon and I were teetering on the edge

of incompetence. We didn't *really* know how to run a restaurant, though we were learning as fast as we could. Jared made us feel taken care of. We could walk in the front door around noon, and he would have already been there for hours, making sauce, slicing mushrooms, grinding the Grana Padano, shaping the dough, toasting thin slices of baguette for me to plate with burrata, a creamy cousin of fresh mozzarella. We could sleep. We didn't have to worry.

There were many weeks that fall when the three of us would eat lunch together every Saturday. Brandon and I would go to the farmers' market to stock the restaurant for the weekend, and while we were there, we would look for something extra, something nice, to share for lunch. Then we'd bring it back to Delancey, and Jared would jump to cook it. It was his chance to show off, and we enjoyed the performance. There might be wood-oven-roasted scallops with white wine, butter, shallots, and parsley, or maybe steamed mussels in a similar treatment. We'd each have a small pour of wine in a crystal glass, the ones we usually save for customers. I remember taking pictures of one of those lunches, because it looked so unreal, like somebody's fantasy of a restaurant owner's life, like something out of a magazine article about Alice Waters. I learned to like oysters when Jared shucked a few Kumamotos one Saturday, made a mignonette, and dared me to try it. I hadn't touched a raw oyster since I was six years old, when my parents offered me one and I nearly gagged on it. Those lunches with Brandon and Jared made me feel like we were a team, and even some kind of family. They made me feel like we were doing something right with Delancey, that Brandon was right in his belief that the restaurant could be an extension of us and everything we cared about.

It was important to us that Jared was happy, because his happiness would mean that we had a good restaurant. Jared's confidence reassured and flattered Brandon, and it calmed me when I felt overwhelmed. I trusted his judgment readily, because unlike the two of us, he looked like he actually knew what he was doing. On days when I was tired or worried, Brandon would try to comfort me, but I didn't want to hear it from him. *You got us into this,* I remember thinking. Jared would get us out of it.

When the restaurant opened, I had a dozen Rolling Stones songs on my iPod, and we listened to them nearly every night. There were a couple of neighborhood high school boys who occasionally picked up dishwashing shifts when our regular dishwasher couldn't come, and whenever we'd get to "Gimme Shelter," they'd look out from under their early-Beatles hair, nod to each other, and without looking up from the dishes, begin playing air guitar in tandem. But before "Gimme Shelter," there was "Angie." She was up first. I would turn on the Stones playlist just before we opened, as we hurried to finish setting up. The door was still shut, but I could see people lining up out front. I would stand at the sink, cranking the handle of the giant green salad spinner that sounded like an airplane taking off, and though I knew I should have been out of my mind with excitement and pride that people were not only coming to our restaurant, but *waiting in line to come to our restaurant,* mostly I felt like we were under siege. I was exhausted. Brandon was exhausted. By this point, even a dental cleaning would have felt like a vacation, just for the opportunity to lie down for an hour. Come five o'clock, I knew, 1415 Northwest 70th Street would become the battle for Minas Tirith, the part when Sauron's army is going after the fortress door with a battering ram shaped like a flaming wolf's head, and the pantry station, my station, would be the first one mauled. So we would turn on the Stones, and "Angie" would build and retreat, and Mick would plead, and everything would feel very clear and poignant, as though I were hovering up near the ceiling, looking down at us. And then the resignation would settle over me: this thing is really happening, and at least we're in it together, the servers and the host and the dishwasher, and me and Brandon and Jared.

TONI'S APPLE CRISP

This is a tweak on my mother's wonderful apple crisp, which is, in turn, based on a recipe from an old family friend named Mimi Smith. The apples wind up sweet-tart and saucy, and there's plenty of crunchy topping. When I was growing up, my mother would make it for dinner parties or holidays, and she always baked it in a soufflé dish. Mimi's original version suggests adding raisins, but my mother never used them, so I don't either.

Note that the recipe also scales up nicely. At Delancey, I always made a double batch, and when the pan was empty, I would scavenge the last crispy bits from the corners before I passed it to the dishwasher.

For the Apples

8 medium Granny Smith apples (1.5 kg, or about 3 pounds)

3 to 4 tablespoons freshly squeezed lemon juice

4 to 6 tablespoons (50 to 75 g) granulated sugar

For the Topping

1 1/2 cups (210 g) unbleached all-purpose flour

1 cup (190 g) brown sugar

2 teaspoons ground cinnamon
1/4 teaspoon fine sea salt
1 1/2 sticks (170 g) unsalted butter, at room
  temperature
1/2 cup (50 g) walnuts, coarsely chopped

For Serving
Heavy cream or vanilla ice cream

Preheat the oven to 350°F. Lightly butter a 2-quart soufflé dish, or grease it with cooking spray. (If you don't have a soufflé dish, an 8 by 8-inch baking dish will stand in nicely.)

Prepare the Apples
Peel, core, and slice each apple into 8 to 10 wedges. In a bowl, toss the apples with 3 tablespoons lemon juice and 4 tablespoons sugar. Taste: they should be bright with lemon but lightly sweet. If needed, add more lemon juice and/or sugar. Scrape the apples and any juices into the prepared dish.

Make the Topping
In a medium bowl, whisk the flour, brown sugar, cinnamon, and salt until evenly combined. Add the butter, and use your fingers to rub and pinch the butter into the dry ingredients until there are no large lumps of butter and the mixture is evenly

crumbly. Add the walnuts, and stir briefly to mix.

To Assemble
Sprinkle the topping evenly over the apples. Bake for 45 to 60 minutes, or until the top of the crisp is lightly browned and the apples are bubbling. Serve warm, with a splash of fresh cream or a scoop of vanilla ice cream.

Yield: 8 servings

19

For the first four months of Delancey's life, Brandon and I were fueled by a potent mixture of lukewarm pizza, chocolate chip cookie dough, elation, and fear. We'd gotten the place open. We were making food for people, and *they actually paid us for it*! Standing next to my husband in the restaurant we'd worked so hard for, I finally understood the kind of insufferable pride that inspires parents of honors students to put bumper stickers on their cars (MY RESTAURANT IS AN HONOR STUDENT . . . ON YELP). There were nights when a customer would stop to hug us on the way out after dinner. There were nights when the bar would be peopled by regulars, strangers who'd become our friends. There were nights when I couldn't imagine being anywhere else. But there were also nights when I wanted to tear off my apron and my clothes and my skin and run, screaming, out the front door.

Great restaurant cooks thrive under pressure. They're performers. They may swear and bitch, but they like the challenge, the intensity, the urgency. Or, if they don't actively *like* it, they at least have the ability to tolerate it. A restaurant cook who is properly equipped for her job, personality-wise and otherwise, is a lot like an athlete. A successful athlete gets a charge out of the challenge, and that's how she's able to cope. I am no athlete — I went out for high school volleyball and wound up as team manager — and I am not a great restaurant cook. I knew that on the June night when I decided to be Delancey's opening pantry cook, but I hoped that I was wrong. I hoped that working in my *own* professional kitchen would make everything different, better. A lot of the time it did. But I couldn't change my temperament. When faced with a dozen orders, I do not get an adrenaline rush. I do what I did on Halloween night of 2009: I cry.

Halloween fell on a Saturday. We'd been officially open for about two and a half months, and we'd had a lot of busy nights, but none of them were as busy as the first seating on Halloween. When we opened the door at five o'clock, there was a long line of families outside, adults and young children in costume, waiting to eat a quick dinner before heading out to trick-or-treat. The entire dining room was seated immediately. That's not all that unusual, and on a typical night, it's not a problem. Only some tables will order starters, while others, especially ones with very young kids, will cut straight to pizza. Tickets land on the pantry cook's station at a measured pace, so that if you're moving at a reasonable clip, you'll rarely wind up "in the weeds," in cooks' lingo. But on Halloween, the servers began bringing me tickets at a few minutes after five, and they didn't stop. By five-fifteen, I had twelve tickets in front of me, each of them for two or three starters.

I began doing mental calculations, adding up how long it would take me to get through them all. It could easily be more than half an hour, I realized, and probably closer to forty-five minutes, before the last table would even see their first course. They had no way to know that every table around them had ordered as much as they had, or that there is only one pantry cook at Delancey. They had no reason to understand the wait. They would be livid. Their offspring, the sneering witches and dead-eyed ghouls, would put a curse on the restaurant.

They would tell everyone they knew how slow and awful Delancey was, that they waited thirty minutes *for a salad.*

After hitting the iceberg, it took the *Titanic* a leisurely two hours and forty minutes to sink. After we opened the doors on Halloween night, it took me fifteen minutes. I stared at the tickets, trying to organize the salads into a few large batches, and then I reached for my biggest bowl, and then I forgot how many batches I had decided on, so I looked at the tickets again, and that was when I started to sniffle. Then I started to cry. I couldn't see very well, so I fumbled and groped my way through the first three salads. Then I looked at the tickets again, and then I started to sob. Jared walked by to get something out of the fridge. Without saying a word, he took down a bowl and started to make the next two salads. Danielle quietly slipped a glass of Champagne onto the shelf above my ticket rail. Between pizzas, Brandon rubbed my shoulders. I spent the rest of the night alternately plating food and hiding in a corner by the chest freezer, wiping my eyes with a paper towel.

A full dining room is a good problem to have, and I was usually grateful to have it. But it's a fine line between eager customers and an angry mob. Ben once told me a story about an opera he directed in the cathedral at the University of Pittsburgh. It's a spectacular Gothic structure, but as it turned out, it didn't have the electrical capacity to support the lighting they had installed. Normally you would open the doors to a performance space at least a half hour before curtain time, but that night, at that point, there were no lights. The front doors had windows, and from the inside, Ben could see a crowd gathering on the other side. And even as he was elated to see it, he felt more and more panicked as each new person appeared, imagining them clawing at the door, wild-eyed, suddenly transformed into the bloody-mouthed zombies from "Thriller." And now, here I was with *actual* zombies in the dining room, and they weren't there to do a dance number with Michael Jackson.

While I sobbed into the greens, I wondered how Brandon, standing a few feet away at the pizza oven, could handle the onslaught of tickets. Answer: he's an East Coaster. In a pinch, he has access to such concepts as *Fuck 'em,* and *Let 'em wait,* and *I'm working as fast as I can here.* I am a people-pleaser from Oklahoma, where life is placid enough that it's considered song-worthy to watch a hawk making lazy circles in the sky.

It's no wonder that the restaurant industry is rife with substance use and abuse. The work depends on adrenaline, the body's natural drug, and when that wears off, there's plenty of the other kind around. There's a bar fridge full of it, to start with. Brandon depends on adrenaline like any other cook, and when it doesn't come, he struggles to get through the night. But he doesn't like the feeling of drinking a lot, and he's never smoked, so his other options are limited. I'm about the same, though once, in my early twenties, I tried smoking weed from a pipe named Colonel Mustard and felt sure that my lungs were collapsing afterward. Brandon believed that there had to be people in the restaurant world who were like us, and that we would find them. I wasn't sure.

Restaurant people, and cooks in particular, are a self-selecting crowd. They have to be able to take not just pressure but also criticism. They must be willing to stand up for eight to sixteen hours a day. They have to enjoy staying up late. Often, they come to the job because they dislike the structures of normal nine-to-five society. Restaurant work means dirty jokes and late-night shots, and it also has the benefit of being one of the few types of employment that allows you to leave your work at work: you clock in, do your hours, and clock out, and then you get to live your life. (Unless, of course, you own the place.) It's not that restaurants are blissfully free of structure and authority; it's just that, in a working kitchen, the authority figure might call you a name that would have your mother reaching for a bar of soap. There's a scene in Anthony Bourdain's *Kitchen Confidential* in which a wedding party goes into a restaurant where Bourdain is working and the bride winds up bent over a trash can in the alley *in her wedding dress,* having sex with a cook. It's extreme, but it says something.

During the first few months after we opened Delancey, a few people told me that it was sad to see me give up my career for my husband. I knew that they meant well, and that it might reasonably look that way. Sure, right: I hadn't chosen to open a restaurant. My husband did that part. But I did, however, choose to work in it. He never asked that of me; I wanted it. I wanted to try it. I wanted to push myself. But when it was clear that I was failing — or clear, anyway, that I couldn't plate a salad if I was crying too hard to see — that's when I wanted out.

MY KATE'S BROWNIES

These brownies were one of the desserts on the Delancey menu on Halloween night, and like the apple crisp, the recipe originally comes from my mother's repertoire. She's been making it for decades. She found the recipe in an article about Katharine Hepburn in a 1975 issue of *The Ladies' Home Journal,* and she always refers to them as Kate's Brownies. In the years since she shared the recipe with me, I've tweaked it slightly, decreasing the sugar and the baking time. The brownies are thin, but they stay chewy and fudgy, and I think they're perfect. At Delancey, I smartened them up with a spoonful of barely sweetened whipped cream, but at home, I like them best plain.

For the record, they're also great when made with white whole wheat flour.

1 stick (113 g) unsalted butter
2 ounces (55 g) unsweetened chocolate, coarsely chopped
1 cup minus 2 tablespoons (175 g) sugar
2 large eggs
1/2 teaspoon vanilla extract
1/4 cup (35 g) unbleached all-purpose flour
1/4 teaspoon fine sea salt

Preheat the oven to 325°F. Lightly butter

an 8-inch square baking dish, or grease it with cooking spray. Cut a rectangle of parchment paper that's long enough to line the bottom and two sides of the dish, leaving a little overhang. Press the parchment paper into the dish. Lightly grease the parchment paper.

In a medium (2 1/2- to 3-quart) saucepan, warm the butter and chocolate over low heat, stirring occasionally, until fully melted. Remove the pan from the heat. Add the sugar, and stir well. The batter will look gritty. Add the eggs and the vanilla, and stir to blend completely. Stir in the flour and salt. The batter should now be very smooth. Pour it into the prepared baking dish, tilting the dish as necessary to ease the batter out into the corners, and then bang the dish straight down on the countertop a couple of times, to release any air bubbles. Place the dish in the oven.

Begin checking the brownies after 25 minutes, inserting a toothpick into the center to test for doneness. They're ready when the toothpick comes out clean. The original version of this recipe says to bake them for 40 minutes, but mine are generally ready between 30 and 35 minutes. When yours are ready, remove the dish from the oven, and allow them to cool completely on a wire rack — and I mean completely, or else they'll be too fragile to cut.

When they're cool, loosen along the edges of the dish with a thin knife, pull up the parchment paper to lift the brownies from the dish, and then cut them into squares.

Yield: 16 squares

20

I went looking just now for a letter I wrote early that November, but I must have gotten rid of it. It was a letter to our staff, informing them that we were closing Delancey. I probably knew that if I didn't delete it, I would have to read it again someday. I'm glad I deleted it.

I remember the date because it was Erin's birthday. She worked for us through the early winter of 2010, when she moved away to go to school. She mostly worked as a host, but she was interested in cooking, too, and was considering doing it professionally one day. So, she picked up the occasional pantry shift for me, which allowed me to sneak a little breathing room and tend to some deadlines. I was two years into a monthly column for *Bon Appétit* then, and the column was supposed to be about home cooking, something I was hardly doing anymore. But it would be months before

Delancey would give us an income, and regular gigs in national magazines come along about as often as Halley's Comet, so I kept at it, and so that I could keep at it, Erin worked my station from time to time. On the night of her birthday, Erin was working and I was at home. The night went well, and Brandon felt good, so after closing and cleaning up, he decided to do something he'd never done before: take the staff to our neighborhood dive bar for a celebratory drink.

That night, Brandon got home late, after two in the morning. He'd called to say that he was going to the bar, but I'd still expected him home earlier. I was lying awake in bed, having paranoid visions of him making out in the bathroom of the bar with a chain-smoker in cut-offs. Between Jared's increasingly erratic behavior and the strain that the long hours were putting on Brandon and me, I was spending time in dark places.

I heard the side door unlatch, and the dog leapt off the bed and ran down the hall. Brandon appeared in the bedroom doorway. He was in tears. Obviously, he *had* cheated on me and was now filled with self-loathing and Jägermeister. He threw himself on the bed, sobbing, and turned away from me. I'm not sure what would have felt worse: if he had cheated, or what actually happened.

"I can't do this," he howled. "It's too hard!" His whole body heaved. "I don't want to do this anymore. I don't want this restaurant."

Two weeks earlier, just before we were due to open for the night, Jared noticed that the recycling hadn't been taken out. Ordinarily, as the day's deliveries come in, the cooks put everything away and then toss the empty cardboard boxes next to the host station, and it's the host's job to break them down and carry them out to the recycling dumpster. It's part of the division of labor in the restaurant, and it's been that way since we opened. But that day in October, as customers waited to come inside, the cardboard boxes were still sitting there. Brandon and I were at the back of the restaurant, working on a batch of vinaigrette. We hadn't noticed the boxes. But Jared noticed, and since the host was busy with something else, he asked Tiffany, a server who was standing nearby, to start breaking them down. Tiffany grabbed a pair of scissors and got to work, but later that night, she came to Brandon about it, complaining, asking if Jared was a manager now, since he was bossing her around.

It was hard for us to fault Jared for what he did. We could see why Tiffany was annoyed, but it was reassuring that Jared had stepped up, that he felt invested enough to care. But we also knew that it wasn't Jared's job to tell Tiffany what to do. The fact that he didn't come to us and let us handle it was a problem, as was the fact that he was defensive when we later spoke to him about it. Mostly, we were annoyed that the two of them were handling it like guests on *The Jerry Springer Show*. Brandon and I had been on our feet all day, and we were not about to march into battle for some empty produce boxes.

On the night of Erin's birthday, the bar was nearly empty. Brandon and the staff slid into a booth and ordered a round, but it was clear that the bartender wanted to close up early. When they'd finished their drinks, Brandon suggested returning to Delancey. So they walked back and helped themselves to beers, and that was when Tiffany decided to revisit the Big Recycling Issue. It was Jared's last day of work for the week, and he'd had a beer or two before the group went to the bar, plus another beer and a shot while they were there.

"You know why I did it?" he said, talking nonchalantly into his glass. "I did it because

I'm above you here. I'm your boss."

Oh, God, Brandon thought. *He's drunk.*

"I'm your boss, Tiffany," Jared repeated.

"Actually," Brandon interrupted, "you're not. You're not anyone's boss."

Jared tossed back the last of his beer, spun off the stool, and threw open the door. Brandon went out after him, but Jared shook him off and disappeared around the corner. When Brandon got back inside, he found the servers laughing, kicking around ripostes to Jared's rant. "Classic back-of-house shit. Cooks are always bullies!" There was no sense in defending Jared, but Brandon was frustrated to hear the servers turn it into a petty case of us-versus-them. *What was the point,* he thought, *of having worked my ass off to open this restaurant if I can't enjoy it? If I can't work with people I like? If we can't even go out for beers together? If I have to deal with* this?

I would like to be able to tell you that I understood, as I lay there while he sobbed. I would like to tell you that I understood that I was supposed to console him. I was supposed to rub his back and tell him that we would be okay. I was supposed to have some perspective — to see that, like every day before this one, today would end and we would make sense of it in the morning.

But it didn't occur to me to do that. I can sit here and see it now — *ah yes, I should have just reached over and held him* — but I've had years to think about it. That night, after having spent months building Delancey, after having spent months working there, after having myself been reduced to a sobbing heap just a week or two earlier, I could not rub his back. He wasn't allowed to say that it was too hard. I didn't care what had happened, or that it was actually, objectively, yes, very, very hard. We had opened this business because he wanted it. He didn't get the privilege of saying that he didn't want to do it anymore.

I told him this, or something like it. I screamed. I remember him asking me over and over why I couldn't understand, why I couldn't just comfort him. He lay there crying while I took my glasses from the nightstand and stood up. I went to the basement, to the storage room that we called our guest bedroom, a collection of boxes with a double bed against one wall. I lay there for a while, trying to get used to what he had told me: *He doesn't want to do this. He wants to close the restaurant. We have to close the restaurant.* I retrieved the computer from my desk upstairs, and lying there in the dark, wrote a letter to our staff to announce

267

Delancey's closure. It was terrible, and it was also a relief.

It never occurred to me that he hadn't meant it. It never occurred to me that he was exhausted, like I was, or that he could reach a breaking point, like I had. It never occurred to me that the next morning, he would wake up, get dressed, and go to work like he always did — that he would still believe in Delancey, and I wouldn't.

21

The summer that I was eighteen, I was killing time in Oklahoma City, waiting to leave
for college, and I killed a lot of it at a Barnes
& Noble bookstore near my parents' house.
These were the days when people still
bought CDs, and the store had a music section in the back. There was a listening station in one corner where you could vet new
arrivals, and one day, an album there caught
my eye. It was *Feelings,* by David Byrne,
the former singer for Talking Heads. I knew
the band the way anyone does, from hear-
ing "Burning Down the House" on the
radio, but *Feelings* was my real introduc-
tion to David Byrne. The thing about David
Byrne is, he's weird. He's weird, but because
he has immense talent, it works. He does
what he wants. He makes music, of course,
but he's also written books about bicycling,
designed art installations that turn buildings into musical instruments and put cloth-

ing on pieces of furniture, delivered lectures-cum-stand-up-routines on the subject of PowerPoint, sung arias by Bizet, and somehow managed to look 100 percent straight while wearing a tutu over his clothes. What I admire most, beyond his sense of humor, is his skill at self-reinvention. It's not that I have a strong desire to dress a table in a pair of pleated chinos, but I like that he's not afraid to try it, and that he's savvy enough to pull it off.

I've always thought it was a little stupid to look up to celebrities. But if I'm going to, it's got to be a celebrity who can teach me something about living authentically without fear, like Byrne, or Animal from the Muppets. When I decided to quit graduate school, I thought of David Byrne. I thought of him when I quit my job in publishing to write my first book. And I was thinking of him when I decided to work at Delancey.

I wanted to be game. I wanted to be able to pull it off. I wanted to surprise myself and Brandon. I'd read these dreamy magazine profiles of husband-wife teams in Brooklyn and San Francisco and Paris, working together to build their artfully conceived boutique business, pickling vegetables or making cupcakes or running a tiny neighborhood restaurant that sat on the cusp of world domination. I pictured myself like those women, with a striped linen apron and dewy, hardworking skin and a hairstyle that said both "I'm too happy to care" and "Brandon and I took a 'nap' [wink, wink] in the office after lunch." *That's the kind of wife I'm going to be,* I decided. *Forget writing. Forget that old restaurant internship, the one that made me think I don't like professional cooking! I'm in the reinvention business!*

I had the striped linen apron, thanks to Carla, who gave me one of hers. I also had the dewy skin, thanks to the lack of an exhaust fan in the kitchen. But as much as I tried to cultivate a devil-may-care attitude and its matching hairdo, I was a miserable wreck.

Brandon has pointed out, and I agree, that we probably wouldn't be married anymore if (1) I hadn't worked at Delancey and (2) I hadn't stopped working at Delancey. I lasted four months in the kitchen, and despite my clear unsuitability for the job, he had to almost shove me out. It took a number of conversations, and most of them went like this:

Brandon: Are you mad about something? I feel like you're grumpy today.

271

Molly: I'm not grumpy. You're grumpy.

Brandon: Hey, you know, you really don't have to do this anymore. You know that, right? If it makes you unhappy, don't do it. Let's get someone else to do it.

Molly: I *can't* not do this. Who's going to do it if I don't?

I knew the answer, of course: we'd put up an ad and hire someone. But that seemed inconceivable. I'd been there since Day One, since before Day One. I knew everything about the place. Who would look after the station, and the restaurant, the way I did? Who would be Brandon's partner? Who would make sure there were no fingerprints on the wine glasses? I was one of the legions of employees who've made the mistake of overestimating their importance to their employer, but the real problem was, I *was* my employer.

We began planning my departure the only way I was willing: very, very slowly. We inched me out. Erin, the host who had sometimes picked up shifts for me, didn't like kitchen work as much as she had hoped to, so she wasn't an option. But our friend Kari, a retired professional ballet dancer and talented cook, was just beginning a career in restaurants, and she'd spent the summer interning at another place in town. In mid-October, she came to us, asking if we had an opening for a paid cooking position. Brandon liked the idea of Kari as a cook because of her background as a dancer: she knew how to work hard and how to pay attention to details. I liked the idea because *we knew her.* I hoped that, because she knew us as people and not just as bosses, she would care about the job, and about Delancey, as much as I did. We offered her two nights a week, her first paid cooking job. I would work the other three nights.

In late October, my cousin Katie and her friend Pantea, Delancey's designers, flew up from the Bay Area to spend a weekend in Seattle and eat at the restaurant. They brought a few girlfriends along, and one of them was an architect-turned-pastry-chef named Brandi Henderson. Their last night in town was a night off for us, so we all went out to dinner, and I wound up talking with Brandi about some problems I was having in coming up with a new fall dessert for the menu. Brandi quickly fired off a few ideas, and then she laughed and added, "Actually, if you ever need a pastry chef, my boyfriend and I have been wanting to move somewhere new. I could come work for you."

I laughed, too. It didn't occur to me that she meant it.

But a few days later, she sent an e-mail to continue the conversation. The e-mail went directly to my spam folder, as did a second e-mail she sent the following week. Luckily, she had the guts to call, asking if she'd used the wrong e-mail address. We'd never tasted any of Brandi's desserts, nor any other food she'd made, but she was smart and energetic and had gone to culinary school, and Katie and Pantea could vouch for her abilities. Like Kari, Brandi knew us first as friends — cousins-of-friends, anyway — and I hoped that meant something. In early November we hired her, and by December 1 she was in Seattle, where she became Delancey's pastry chef and part-time pantry cook, since the positions overlapped.

I spent my last shifts training Brandi. I was so obsessive about it that I even showed her how to whip cream, as though she'd never done it before. She politely watched and listened and repeated after me, and if she thought I was an idiot, she kept it to herself. I liked her. I also liked the Meyer lemon *budino* that she suggested for the dessert menu, with anise caramel, candied pistachios, and sablé cookies. Because of

Brandi and Kari, who'd recently come up with a beautiful salad of roasted beets, three types of citrus, and ricotta salata, I could leave.

Suddenly, I was done. For the next few weeks, I could hardly go to the restaurant. The instant I walked in, I'd see something that needed doing. I'd be sucked in, compelled to do it. I hated the restaurant for that, for the fact that red pepper flakes get wedged into crevices in the tabletops and flour gets everywhere. It was all I could see: the dirt, the problems, the trouble. On the days that the restaurant was closed, Brandon mostly slept, and when we closed for our first long break over the holidays, he promptly came down with a virus. I had visions of us making eggnog together like we had the year before, my great-grandfather's profoundly boozed-up eggnog, and cooking every night, the way we used to. But we'd stopped cooking at home, both together and separately, months before, and a few days off wasn't going to bring it back.

When my first book came out earlier that year and I did a reading in New York, my editor took me to dinner. I was so nervous that I hardly remember what the place looked like, or how we got from the front door to our booth. I had met my editor in person only once before, and I still sort of didn't believe that I had managed to write a book at all. I worried that if I opened my mouth, she would figure me out. We drank a bottle of Champagne that she ordered, and mostly we talked about Delancey, which was then under construction. I didn't know yet that I would work there — it was still solidly Brandon's project — but my editor asked me something that I've revisited many times since. *What will it be like for you,* she said, *to make cooking a public thing? It's always been a part of your private life, even though you write about it. What will it be like for you and Brandon to make it public?*

I'd never thought about it. She had a point: my normal life found me at home, at my desk or in front of the electric range in my small, quiet kitchen, not standing in a restaurant, tending to the needs of strangers. But I didn't know how to answer her. I wouldn't know until after I had left my post at Delancey and was trying to find that normal life again, that in taking cooking from our private world and sharing it with our public one, we would change it. We would lose it.

In the months after I stopped working at Delancey, I thought about cooking, but I rarely did it. I wondered what had happened to me, why I'd gotten so lazy. It's not that I was an elaborate cook before, the type to routinely make three courses on a weeknight — on the contrary, our most frequent meal has always been a big salad, some cheeses, and bread, which can barely even be called cooking — but now I could hardly motivate myself to wash a head of lettuce. I would beat myself up for it, but that didn't change the fact that I didn't want to cook. I was now on my own, at home alone, five nights a week. And on Brandon's days off, we didn't want to make dinner. That was work now, and we wanted to be taken care of. It would be years before we would find a rhythm again — before I would accept that we might never play together in the kitchen the way we used to, every night and every day, before I could look at our marriage without seeing a hole in it. I wondered when we'd go back to being the old, better us. I wondered when I'd go back to being the old, better me.

In an article in the *New York Times* a couple of years ago, Jonathan Franzen talked about what he calls the problem of actual love. "My friend Alice Sebold," he wrote, "likes to talk about 'getting down in the pit and loving somebody.' She has in mind the dirt that love inevitably splatters on the mirror of our self-regard." I've thought about that line a lot. I wanted so much to enjoy this successful thing that Brandon and I had made together, to celebrate his enthusiasm and his hard work. But that's not who I was, or who I could be at that point. It was an ugly thing to see that in the mirror.

Because I loved him, I had encouraged him, even when it scared me. I had wanted to believe in what he believed. I had wanted to help him succeed, because helping him succeed would help us succeed. I had tried to do something that I couldn't do, and it had made me someone who said things and did things I didn't like at all. It made me lash out when I should have put an arm around his shoulder. It made me cry at the thought of making salad. I had not been the person I thought I was: someone fair, someone in control, someone deserving of love. All I had tried to do was be a restaurant cook; it wasn't like I was hoping to sing an aria or make a building play music. But I had failed, and now I didn't know how to go back to what I had been before.

J. P. HARTT'S EGGNOG

My maternal great-grandfather, John Phillip Hartt, came up with this recipe, and my mother's family has made it for decades. Though Brandon didn't grow up with a family nog tradition, he now looks forward to it as much as I do.

This eggnog is a little thinner in texture than most, which I prefer, and alcohol-wise, it's all business. J. P. Hartt made his nog using double the quantities listed below, but because I don't know anyone with a bowl big enough for that, I've scaled it down. You'll still have plenty to go around.

If you're concerned about the raw eggs, I can tell you that alcohol does inhibit bacterial growth — although it cannot, in truth, be relied upon to *kill* bacteria. It may, but I can't make any promises. We make this eggnog with fresh eggs from a local farm that we trust, but if you'd prefer, feel free to use pasteurized eggs.

6 large eggs
1 cup (200 g) sugar
2 1/2 quarts (2 1/3 l) half-and-half
1 fifth (750 ml) brandy
1 cup (240 ml) dark rum
1/2 cup (120 ml) bourbon
1/2 cup (120 ml) dry sherry

1/2 teaspoon nutmeg, preferably freshly grated

In a very large mixing bowl, whisk the eggs to break up the yolks. Add the sugar, and whisk vigorously (or beat with a handheld electric mixer) until the mixture is foamy and lightens a bit in color. Add the half-and-half, whisking (or beating) to combine. Add the brandy, rum, bourbon, and dry sherry, mixing thoroughly. Whisk in the nutmeg, and chill well before serving.

Yield: About 1 gallon

22

I would very much like to tell you that we fired Jared after the "Tiffany, I'm your boss" debacle, and that it was so anticlimactic, so obvious, so *boring,* that I forgot to mention it. That would be significantly less embarrassing. But the truth is, Jared outlasted me at my own restaurant.

He lasted long enough to, among other things, imagine or fabricate an attraction between Brandon and Kari.

"He's sweet on her," Jared told me casually, almost absentmindedly, as though he were recounting what he ate for breakfast. It was late November, and he and I were unpacking a produce delivery together.

I was too tired to question it. I swallowed it whole. Later that night, I confronted Brandon, already set in my refusal to hear his reply. He was incredulous, furious that I believed Jared. Weeks would pass before I was ready to listen. But it never occurred to me, or to Brandon, to fire Jared for it.

We knew that Jared was different from who he had been when we hired him a few months earlier, but we didn't yet know the dimensions of his drinking, or how nasty he was with the rest of the staff when we weren't around. No matter how much your employees like you, when there's a problem among them, they will whisper amongst themselves for weeks — and maybe even months — before reporting it to you. As far as we could see, Jared was a good cook and a reliable employee with a few notable personality issues. I was too busy imploding, and Brandon was too busy working, and we were both too busy trying to learn to run a restaurant to see how bad things had actually gotten. You don't know what to expect, anyway, until you've been at it for a while. I figured that Jared's behavior was typical for a talented, ambitious cook, the type with aspirations to be a Chef-with-a-capital-C. It's the kind of behavior that makes dollar signs appear in the eyes of *Top Chef* producers.

That year, Christmas and New Year's Eve fell in the middle of the workweek, so we decided to close for both weeks, to make the most of it and get some rest. The day before the restaurant reopened, a Tuesday,

Jared stopped by to pick up his paycheck. Brandon and I were there, organizing paperwork and getting ready for the coming week. Jared was hoping to move to a new apartment soon, he explained, and did we think we might be able to float him a loan? A few thousand dollars? I told him the truth: that I was in the process of putting together a bundle of end-of-year reports and receipts to send to our bookkeeper, and that until she'd gone through it, we wouldn't know where we stood, money-wise. We'd been open for barely five months, and there was still debt to pay off, plus upcoming tax deadlines. Could he check back in a month? He agreed.

The next morning, Brandon went to the restaurant to help Jared break down a few pork shoulders for the week's supply of sausage. I was at home, trying to get back into some kind of writing routine. Within half an hour of his departure, the phone rang. It was Brandon.

"Jared's gone," he said by way of a greeting. "I let him go." He sounded calm, matter-of-fact. I thought I could even hear him grinning. It was barely noon on the first day back from our first holiday closure, and we had no pizza cook, and Brandon was all right.

Jared had asked again about the loan, he reported, and he'd also asked for a 150 percent raise, effective immediately.

"I'd be happy to consider some kind of raise at some point," Brandon had told him, "but like we said yesterday, we can't do anything until we know where we are financially."

"I'm worth just as much now as I will be in a month," Jared had retorted.

"Listen, we can't do it right now. And a hundred fifty percent is *a lot.* I can't pay anyone that much."

"Okay," Jared had said, putting down his knife. "Then I'm done."

We didn't have to fire him. We didn't have to wonder what to do. He had made demands that were unreasonable, satisfyingly and undeniably unreasonable, and when we didn't give in, he left. It felt almost easy. I *whooped* into the phone. After we hung up, Brandon made a couple of calls to find someone to fill in for the week, and then he called Ryan Thompson.

The previous summer, one day in early June, Brandon was at Delancey, doing whatever construction task he was doing that week, and a guy showed up and introduced himself. Ryan was in his mid-thirties, a little older than we were, and had put himself through graduate school by working for Punch, a well-known pizzeria in Minnesota. He'd been a cook and then a manager, helping to open new locations. Now he was between careers, working at a pizza shop in Seattle and planning a move to Sonoma in late July, to try working a season at a winery.

Ryan was living at his sister's place, not far from Delancey, and she'd read somewhere about what we were doing. He liked the sound of it, so he rode over on his bike to check it out. He told Brandon that if he needed any help with construction, he'd be happy to pitch in. What kind of stranger does that? Ryan Thompson.

One afternoon not long after, Ryan came back. He and Brandon opened some beers, sat down at the bar, and set to work assembling the pendant lights that were to hang over it. They're made from tall, narrow canning jars meant for asparagus, with a hole drilled in the bottom for an electrical cord to slide through. Katie and Pantea designed them, and our friend Mark, who owns a metal shop, made steel sleeves to slip inside one end of the jar, holding the socket and bulb in place. Each light has a half-dozen parts, and they're not complicated. But when the electrician later went to install them, he had to take apart and re-assemble most of them, because Brandon and Ryan had been so absorbed in talking pizza that they'd botched the whole operation.

Ryan came back nearly every week, and he and Brandon began to practice baking pizzas. Ryan knew a lot about wood-burning ovens, and he showed Brandon some tricks for getting the fire right. Like Brandon, Ryan is fascinated with the details that make food taste the way it does, and that make some versions taste better than others: not only pizza, but also coffee, bourbon, and wine. He knew a hell of a lot more about wine than we did. When the time came to choose the wines for our opening menu, he helped us sift through the samples that our reps brought by and build a list.

We wanted him to stay and work for us. But he wanted to learn about winemaking, and he had that job waiting in California. He left in late July. He e-mailed sometimes to check in and send cheers, and just before the holidays, he wrote to say that he was trying to decide what to do next, that he felt torn between Sonoma and Seattle. Did we have an opening at Delancey? I wrote back to say that we didn't, but that, as we were discovering, the situation could always change. Three weeks later, within twenty minutes of Jared's departure, Brandon was on the phone with Ryan. Ryan packed his car, and four days later, he arrived in Seattle to be our new pizza cook.

He lived with us for a month, in the guest room in our basement. The three of us shared the small bathroom on the main floor. He never used the sheets and comforter we gave him; he just laid his sleeping bag on top of the bed. He worked the prep shift three mornings a week, and four nights a week, he worked the pizza station with Brandon. On Sunday nights, his night off, he and I would cook together if he wasn't spending time with his sister. It was the first real cooking I'd done since leaving my post at Delancey. I was grateful to have company, to have someone other than myself to feed, a reason to get back in the habit. It was midwinter, very cold and wet, and the first night, we decided to braise some short ribs. Neither of us had ever had Yorkshire pudding, but since we had plenty of beef drippings, we decided to make a batch, and that, we discovered, gave us an excuse for talking in faux British accents over dinner. (*What ho!*) It had been months since I'd spent an evening with a friend that way, not working or at the restaurant, just eating and sitting around. Ryan gave me that, along with something else that I also needed: a friend who knew me best within the life we had now, not the life we'd had before the restaurant. I didn't have to explain.

Even after he'd found an apartment of his own and moved out, Ryan would sometimes come over on weekend mornings, and the three of us would make breakfast. One Sunday, we had a French toast cook-off, *Cook's Illustrated*'s recipe versus my father's. (I am pleased to report that the latter won.) Other weekends we did waffles, buckwheat pancakes, or oatmeal pancakes. I would make coffee, mostly badly, and we'd listen to the blues show on KEXP. Or if we weren't making breakfast, we'd meet up for lunch — often giant, sloppy slow-roasted pork sandwiches that I would pick up at a shop called Paseo. Brandon and I have always tended to share close friends: Sam, Ben, Olaiya. During the months that he worked at Delancey, Ryan was the closest person to us. His friendship was the first thing to come out of the restaurant that felt familiar, that felt like *mine*, that I would miss if it disappeared.

As it turned out, Ryan had not only left Sonoma on a moment's notice for us, but he had also left behind a girlfriend, Ana, a winemaker he'd been dating for a couple of months. When he told us, we couldn't believe that he'd come at all. Once every other month or so, she'd fly up to visit, or he'd fly down to see her. In the late spring, April or early May, we congratulated him when he told us that he wanted to go back to Sonoma to be with her. He stayed at Delancey until Memorial Day, and before he left, he helped us to find and train his replacement, a cook his sister knew.

Almost a year after he moved away, Ryan and his girlfriend came to visit. We'd just bought our house, the definition of a fixer-upper. She and I spent an entire afternoon crouched on the living room floor with pliers, yanking up carpet staples, while Ryan and Brandon hauled out the remnants of a wall we'd torn down. We'd run out of furnace oil the day after closing, so the house was very cold, and I have a picture of beautiful, kind Ana in the living room that day, wearing a down parka and work gloves, covered in dust. I came across it again while moving some boxes a few months ago, and it occurred to me that without the mess Jared made, I might not have known her at all.

■ ■ ■ ■

Jared came back once. It was December of 2011, almost two years after his exit. He showed up in the doorway one night, just before opening. I was at home, and Brandon called as soon as Jared left.

"You're not going to believe who was just here," he said. "He came in with a girlfriend and their newborn baby. The girls think he looks like a bearded version of Charlize Theron in *Monster*. But he seems like he's doing really well."

"*He is?* He's doing well?"

"Yeah. Lives in California now. He's got some land there. Grows medical marijuana for a living."

"He's growing marijuana for a living?"

I'm kind of sorry that I wasn't there.

SWEET-HOT SLOW-ROASTED PORK SHOULDER

This roast is quite different from the pork shoulder that Paseo puts in their sandwiches, but in many ways, I like it more. All credit for this recipe goes to Allison Halley, a very talented cook who once worked at Delancey. This roast was inspired by one that Al and her boyfriend, Jason, served at her birthday party. Afterward, at the restaurant, she and Brandon played with seasonings, deciding on a combination similar to that used for the classic Italian roast *porchetta,* and devised a combination smoking/ roasting technique for cooking it. At home, though, I keep it simple and just roast the thing. This isn't the quickest recipe on Earth — the pork should ideally be seasoned twelve to twenty-four hours before cooking, and then it cooks for nearly seven hours — but there's nothing difficult about it, and the result is a tender, hugely flavorful roast with lots of fragrant juices. We happily eat it on its own, with vegetables and some rice or potatoes for sopping up the juices, though it's also terrific in Vietnamese Rice Noodle Salad (page 95) and the leftovers make a killer fried rice (page 169).

You'll want to look for a roast that's well marbled, and if it isn't already tied, ask your butcher to tie it for you. Note that, like the meatloaf on page 119, this recipe is a good reason to keep powder-free latex gloves around. The smell of garlic powder tends to cling to bare skin a little longer than most of us would like. (And in case you wonder, we use garlic powder here because fresh garlic has a tendency to burn.)

1 tablespoon dried thyme leaves
1 tablespoon freshly ground black pepper
1 1/2 teaspoons red pepper flakes
1 1/2 teaspoons garlic powder
One 3-pound (1 1/3 kg) boneless pork
  shoulder roast
1/4 cup (50 g) sugar
1/4 cup (60 ml) fish sauce
Crunchy sea salt, such as Maldon or fleur
  de sel

A day or two before you'd like to serve the roast, season it: Combine the dried thyme, black pepper, and red pepper flakes in a spice grinder or mortar and pestle. Grind thoroughly. Add the garlic powder, and process or stir briefly to combine. Place the roast in a bowl or on a deep plate — something big enough to hold the roast and catch any juices. Rub the roast evenly with the seasoning mixture; then cover the bowl with plastic wrap and refrigerate for 12 to 24 hours.

When you're ready to cook the roast, position a rack in the lower third of the oven and preheat the oven to 200°F.

Remove the roast from the refrigerator, and put it in an enameled cast-iron pot with a lid (I use a 5-quart Dutch oven). Cover the pot, and put it in the oven. Roast the pork — resisting the urge to open the oven to check on it! — until it is fully tender and a lot of juices have accumulated in the bottom of the pot, about 6 hours. (If you check it with a meat thermometer at this point, the center of the roast should read between 170° and 190°F.)

In a small bowl, combine the sugar and fish sauce to make a glaze, whisking until the sugar is dissolved. Remove the pot from the oven, set the lid aside, and pour half of the glaze over the roast. Raise the oven temperature to 225°F, and return the pot, uncovered, to the oven. Cook for 20 minutes more; then pour on the rest of the glaze. Cook for another 20 minutes. By this point, the roast should be nicely browned on top. Remove the roast from the oven, and allow it to rest for at least 10 to 15 minutes before slicing.

You can either slice it thin or cut it into

coarse chunks, depending on how you plan to serve it: slices are lovely when you're serving it on its own, and chunks are a nice way to eat it with rice. In either case, spoon some of the juices from the pot over the pork, sprinkle it lightly with crunchy sea salt, and serve hot.

Yield: about 6 servings

23

I remember the months when I cooked at Delancey — the way it felt to stand at my station in the early afternoon, hovering over the day's to-do list with a Sharpie — as though they ended yesterday. But after I fired myself, each day blurred into the next. I guess that's how it works. When we retell the details of our lives, most of us are no better than the average Yelp reviewer, the one who vividly remembers that the server tipped over a glass of wine but forgets that she comped the entire bottle in apology.

The months after were a lot like the months before: I didn't know what to do with myself. I helped with hiring and training, cleaning and running errands, and I still did payroll and staff scheduling. I did co-owner stuff, manager stuff, the boring stuff that I somehow like. But as much as I could, I stayed away — because even then, even though I wasn't technically working a job there, Delancey always asked for more.

When Brandon wrote the business plan, the business plan that I had been too disbelieving to look at, he had budgeted for the restaurant to be open only forty-eight weeks a year. Europeans get a month of paid vacation, he figured, and so do workers in plenty of other countries. What's the point of taking on the risks of running your own business if you can't step away every once in a while and enjoy what you've built? He made his projections with that in mind, with the idea that the restaurant would generate no income for four weeks of each year. We would make less money, and so would our staff — a fact that could cause insurrection — but nonetheless, he hoped that we could manage it.

In late May of 2010, we decided to take our first proper vacation — not the kind of sleeping-and-seeing-family vacation we'd had over the holidays. This time, we would do it right. We would go somewhere far away, somewhere with good food, somewhere that would return us ready for the hard work of summer, the busy season. We made plans to fly to Paris with two friends, rent an apartment, and spend a week. We were on a budget, so the four of us rented a one-bedroom and crammed into it, with

Brandon and me on the pullout couch in the living room. We ate, and we ate, and we ate well. At the end of the week, Brandon flew home to reopen the restaurant.

Because a plane ticket from Seattle to Europe is never cheap, we agreed that I might as well stay on for another week and get the most out of it. So when he went home, I went to London to visit a friend.

My friend Brian, normally a New Yorker, was living in London that year, and he'd offered me his guest room. My goals were specific: to walk all over the city, and to eat at the River Café, the Michelin-starred restaurant opened by Rose Gray and Ruth Rogers almost twenty-five years prior, a place famous for its refined Italian food and the celebrated cooks (Jamie Oliver, April Bloomfield, Hugh Fearnley-Whittingstall, among others) who learned their trade in its kitchen. I have no patience for the cult of the celebrity chef, but a place with that kind of longevity and success has to be doing something interesting. I wanted to see what it was all about.

Brian made a reservation and invited our mutual friend Charlotte to join us. One very hot Saturday afternoon, the three of us went for lunch. I remember the date: June 5, 2010. There's an L-shaped outdoor patio that runs along the length of the restaurant and then makes a hard left into a garden area, and we were seated in its elbow, under an awning, next to a door that led into the kitchen. We ordered a pitcher of Pimm's Cup — that's what you do, I was learning, in England in the summertime — and a few dishes to share. Servers would emerge from the kitchen every few minutes, carrying plates of food — pink scampi still in their shells, a whole roasted fish on a raft of fennel fronds, a pristine globe of strawberry sorbet in a glass bowl — and we watched them pass, hoping we'd ordered well. After a little while, our antipasti came out, and then fat scallops with grilled polenta, and prosciutto draped over wedges of the summer's first melons. It was all very, very good. Then the pasta course arrived.

We were in mid-conversation when the server presented it, and I remember noticing, as she set down the serving plate, that it was not especially pretty. I'm not looking for my food to resemble an architectural model, but when you're dining in a famous restaurant, I don't know — I just didn't expect the pasta to be ugly. It was listed on the menu as tagliarini with nettles, borage, Parmigiano-Reggiano, butter, and nutmeg, but it looked like a small bird's nest that had been rained on a few times, blown out of its tree, soaked in an algae-filled pond, blotted briefly, and then stepped on. I took a bite.

It tasted much better than it looked. The flavor was quiet at first, the way a train is when you just begin to see it down the track, but a few chews in, the bright green, minerally taste of the nettle came on, and it hung there for a while, ricocheting around my mouth the way the flavor of an oyster does. Even after I swallowed, it was still there, ringing. Brian and Charlotte were talking, so I took a second bite. The flavor filled my entire head, and there's no way to describe what that felt like, except to say that I knew something terrible was about to happen. I was going to cry. I clamped my lips together to stop it, but I must have looked odd, because Brian glanced at me in mid-sentence and then froze, staring, and the way a cork pops out of a Champagne bottle, I let loose a sob.

I feel compelled to assure you that I had never before cried over food, or not since I was in diapers. Not bad food, and certainly not good food. I thought people were moved to tears by food only in movies about famine or in films set in Tuscany with an original soundtrack by Enya. I love food, but I'd never cried about it. And it's not that I was really crying *about* the pasta, per se. Except that I was. I was wiping my eyes with the tablecloth and wheezing.

I hoped maybe it wasn't actually happening, that the unusually hot weather was causing me to sweat profusely from my eyes. Either way, it was a bad place to be doing whatever I was doing. It occurred to me that I might not be able to stop. My friends looked alarmed.

"I'm just so . . . [*wheeze*] . . . moved . . . by this pasta [*wheeze,*]" I managed to get out. And my blubbering made me laugh, and then I wheezed again, and then we were all laughing.

The meal went on, because we had ordered more, and we ate that whole roasted fish, and a loquat tart and an *affogato,* and by the time we were ready to leave, it was nearly four in the afternoon.

As we paid the check, we watched the lunch crew set up their staff meal, a buffet along the bar. They filled their plates and began to stream past us to a lawn next to the patio, where they sat together, at least twenty of them, to eat. They smiled and gestured and leaned into each other, and the whole scene was eminently civilized, idyllic, the kind of vignette you find in an

M. F. K. Fisher essay about a restaurant in the French countryside in the first half of the last century. I couldn't stop staring at them, watching the way they were with each other, the way they clearly enjoyed being there. As they sat, we watched the dinner staff arrive: the servers polishing wine glasses, the female chef taking a seat at the table next to ours with a pencil and a binder stuffed with notes and old menus. *These people,* I thought, *are making something here.* It sounds obvious when I write it down, but that's what I thought: *These people know, and they care, that what they're making is beautiful. They aren't just going through the motions; they're* going after *it.* It was spectacular to watch: calm, precise, quietly exuberant.

I noticed, as I sat there staring, that their routines and patterns — the small, self-contained world they inhabited — felt familiar to me. A year before, it would have meant nothing. But now I understood what they were doing, what motivated them, and why it mattered. I understood their work — how good it can feel to dream up a plate of food and put it on a menu and serve it to people, and how good it feels to sit together afterward and eat and rest and crack a joke — and I *liked* that I understood.

I've never been much of a joiner. I like to be alone. I belonged briefly to my high school's Environmental Club, and once, in college, went to a Ralph Nader Super Rally, but there are few groups in which I've felt a real sense of membership. But watching the daily rituals of this restaurant thousands of miles from our own, I suddenly felt like a part of Delancey. I felt like a part of Brandon. I felt like a part of the small, self-contained world that we had made: one that I had never planned on, that I struggled to negotiate, but that was ours now, mine.

When I was in college, my father used to send me clippings from the *New Yorker*. He would see an article on a topic that I was interested in, or might have been interested in sometime in the previous ten years — he was always slow to notice that his child's interests had evolved, that classic dad trait — and he would fold it up and put it in an envelope and mail it to me. Toward the end of my freshman year, in June of 1998, he sent an article about Jack Kerouac, a collection of excerpts from Kerouac's journal. About six years earlier, when I was in my early teens, I'd been a Kerouac fan. I'd read *On the Road* and had decided to become a Beat poet. Six years later, I had not become a Beat poet, but I read that *New Yorker* article anyway, and something at the end caught me. It was a paragraph from a journal entry that Kerouac wrote shortly before his twenty-eighth birthday, and in it he made a list of pledges to himself, changes and improvements that he wanted to make in anticipation of getting a year older. He vowed to travel more, to sleep less, to take his coffee black, to do chin-ups. Then he wound up his arm and threw down: "You have to believe in life before you can accomplish anything. That is why dour, regular-houred, rational-souled State Department diplomats have done nothing for mankind. Why live if not for excellence?"

I cut that out, that paragraph, and taped it to the wall of my dorm room, and to the wall of every room I've lived in since. Today it's pinned to the wall behind my desk. I don't know exactly what part of it grabbed me twelve years ago, other than the fact that I was in my twenties, like Kerouac, and that I was into being a good student. Being excellent was important to me. Whatever it meant then, it was that dowdy word *excellence,* that word in the Jack Kerouac sense, that came to me at the River Café. Maybe that was why I'd been such a failure of a pantry cook: because I had wanted so much to excel, to please our customers and to succeed, that it had paralyzed me. I couldn't put my head down and just do my job. It was also, I realized, what had made Brandon want to make pizza, and to open Delancey. And it was what kept him awake some nights, regretting a lone sub-par pie that he had tiredly let go out to a customer. His determination, his perfectionism, his dreams for Delancey — they weren't just some maddening obsession; excellence was what he wanted and why he did what he did. We wanted the same thing. I had to wheeze over a plate of pasta in another restaurant, in another country, before I could see that, and before I could see him.

BRANDI'S COCONUT RICE PUDDING

It was cherry season when I got back to Seattle, and Brandi, Delancey's pastry chef, had developed this pudding as a way to show them off: a small bowl of cold coconut rice pudding, topped with macerated fresh cherries from the farmers' market and a dusting of crunchy coconut streusel. It's good enough that one of the servers [*cough, cough,* Katie] once ate so much that she got "the sweats." But the rice pudding is delicious on its own, too, and that's how I like it at home. If you'd like to try it with cherries, though, just halve and pit them, and then toss them gently with sugar and lemon juice — about 1 tablespoon of sugar and 1 teaspoon of lemon juice for every 6 ounces (170 g) of cherries.

Canned coconut milk is available in most grocery stores, but be sure not to buy the reduced-fat kind. This recipe is best made with full-fat coconut milk. If you're having dessert, I figure, have dessert — fat, sugar, the real stuff.

3/4 cup (135 g) basmati rice
1 1/2 cups (350 ml) water, plus more for
    washing the rice
1/4 teaspoon fine sea salt
2 cups (475 ml) coconut milk

2 cups (475 ml) whole milk
1 cup (235 ml) heavy cream
1/2 cup plus 1 tablespoon (112 g) sugar
Half a vanilla bean

Put the rice in a medium bowl, add cold water to cover, and swish the rice around with your fingers to remove the excess starch. Drain, and repeat two more times.

In a heavy large (4-quart) saucepan, combine the 1 1/2 cups water, the washed rice, and the salt. Place over medium-high heat. When the water begins to simmer, cover the pan and reduce the heat to low. Simmer until the water is absorbed, about 10 minutes. Then stir in the coconut milk, 1 cup of the whole milk, the cream, and the sugar. Scrape in the seeds from the vanilla bean, and then add the pod as well. Raise the heat to medium and continue to cook, uncovered, stirring occasionally, until the rice is tender and the mixture thickens to a soft, creamy texture, about 35 minutes. Remove from the heat, and discard the vanilla pod. Stir in the remaining 1 cup whole milk.

Transfer the pudding to a storage container. Press a sheet of plastic wrap directly onto its surface, to prevent a skin from forming. Refrigerate until thoroughly chilled.

Serve the pudding in small bowls, with cherries, if you like.

Yield: 8 to 12 servings

24

Like toddlers and sharks, a restaurant never holds still. One day, it might seem that you've got it pinned down, figured out, every problem solved, but the next day, a prep cook will forget to put salt in the pizza dough, the freezer will be found unplugged, and water will start dripping from the ceiling of the walk-in. We have days, and weeks, like that. But as the months passed, Delancey began to really *work,* in every sense of the word. I never thought I would say it — in fact, I have blushed at the naïveté of even thinking of saying it — but sometimes, Delancey does feel like a dinner party. Nobody wears a chef's toque, and nobody cares how precisely you can *brunoise* a carrot. But everybody wants to cook a good meal, and to do it in good company. Our staff calls it "the pizza party."

This industry that seemed so *other* turned out to involve a lot of people like us.

Granted, it takes real work to find them. There are plenty of the other kind to choose from, and plenty of people who want to hire them. The other day, I came upon an online ad posted by a chef who was looking to hire a "sick" baker for his restaurant. "One of those really crazy, socially off ones," he specified, "that make line cooks seem sane." I'll bet his in-box was full within the hour.

We set a certain tone at Delancey. Articles in business magazines call it "workplace culture," a concept so dull-sounding, so soporific, that you could use it as the basis for a lullaby. But Brandon and I spend a lot of time at Delancey, and we need it to feel like a pleasant place to be. And it turns out that even if you want a workplace that's fairly unstructured and relaxed, it takes guiding, shaping, and difficult conversations to get there. After a while, we came around to Susan the Oracle's method of hiring, often choosing fed-up paralegals, ex-dancers, and part-time choreographers over professionally trained cooks. To do well at Delancey, you've got to like collaboration. The restaurant is small, and we don't have a dozen bussers and interns to do the grunt work: everyone has to do their part, and sometimes more. You can't keep score. You've got to take initiative, to do your job well for the sake of doing it well. In return, we'll be game to hear your ideas, and to help you to learn what you want to learn. A couple of years ago, when one of our cooks wanted to start curing meat, we brought in a chef-instructor from the local culinary school to teach him. Now you can get your Delancey pizza with house-made lardo, coppa, or bresaola.

But there are exceptions, and we still make mistakes. Last year we hired a new cook, a very experienced cook who came recommended. He'd been working in fine dining and was eager for a change. He wanted a more mellow, lighthearted environment, he said. He worked for a week before giving notice. Our kitchen was too unstructured, he told one of the other cooks, and he missed the formality and straightforward heirarchy of a traditional kitchen.

I was talking the other day with my friend Matthew, and he said something that surprised me. He said that, as a customer, Delancey has always felt the same to him — that from his seat at the bar, he never saw the big ups and downs. It was a relief to hear — maybe no one noticed the streaky wine glasses that gave me night sweats? — but it surprised me. The whole restaurant

311

has surprised me, and maybe the people in it most of all. Sometimes I come in late at night, just before closing, and Brandon and I sit at the bar and share a pizza and a couple of beers. We watch the kitchen's final hustle, the servers clearing tables and filling the mop bucket, and I think, *Hey, whoa, we did it. This place was once an empty room covered in popcorn-ceiling debris. Now we provide jobs for fifteen people! Fifteen people who like this place enough to hang out here on their days off! Fifteen people we like enough to call friends!* The staff and many of the regulars, they're now the people we spend our time with — not because we have to, but because we do. It was a community that we fell into, and then one that we chose.

It's hard to talk about any of this without veering into sticky, sappy territory. Actually, what I should apologize for is the fact that I can't talk about it without referencing an early '90s romantic comedy starring Matt Dillon. It's *Singles,* a Cameron Crowe movie, the story of a group of twenty-something, grunge-era Seattleites looking for love. I'm a big *Singles* fan. In particularly low moments, I even quote lines from it. It's not that it's a great film (though I think it's a very good one) or a particularly accurate portrayal of my adopted city (grunge had already gone the way of the cassette tape by the time I arrived), but I am to *Singles* as pre-teen boys are to *Monty Python and the Holy Grail:* I know it backward and forward, as though it were made expressly for me. About midway through, when Kyra Sedgwick's character is dating Campbell Scott's character, she walks into the coffee shop where he often hangs out. As she enters, the camera shoots from her point of view, slowly scanning the faces of the movie's other major characters, who are all in the coffee shop too, as they greet her. That's what it's like when I walk into Delancey to meet Brandon for a late dinner after service. I'm Kyra Sedgwick — indulge me here — and over there, there's Katie, who's been with us since two months after Delancey opened; Jenn, who started in the spring of 2010; Mariko, who started not long after Jenn; Estela, who filled in as a dishwasher one day in late 2010 and is still around today; Brandi, still steering the dessert menu; and Joe, Brandon's right-hand pizza man for two years. There's the couple of regulars who come in once a week and bring us homemade jam in the summer, another couple whose dog is our dog's best friend, the neighbor who called once to tell us that he'd caught a salmon and wanted to give us half; the pair of ladies who got married at the table by the bar.

Sam fills in sometimes as a host. For a time, he ran his web design business out of Delancey's back office. Megan Gordon, his girlfriend, made her wildly popular Marge Granola in the Delancey kitchen for more than a year, baking it on days when we're closed. In the summer of 2011, Brandi teamed up with Olaiya to found the Pantry at Delancey, a cooking school and community kitchen located directly behind the restaurant. Rachel Marshall, who worked for us as a server from late 2009 until late 2011, made and bottled her eponymous ginger beer at Delancey until the stuff became so successful that she took it full-time, building her own production kitchen and opening a bar called Montana and a Rachel's Ginger Beer shop at Pike Place Market. Though our friends could be successes anywhere, it's been nice to do it together, to have the company, to be able to hoist each other up.

Almost a decade ago, when I decided to quit graduate school, I was newly broken up with a boyfriend. He was a very kind, serious, thoughtful guy, someone who tutors kids with severe learning disabilities in his free time. I remember feeling so frivolous in comparison, so guilty, as I thought about giving up academia to try being a food writer. Food writing wasn't important. It wouldn't save a life. I did it anyway, because I wanted to, but I certainly couldn't justify it on the grounds of world peace. That justification doesn't work for opening a restaurant either. But there is something about Delancey that, to me, matters just as much: We get to make people happy. We get to give people a good night. We get to spend our days doing work that we can be proud of, and when we're done, there's all the pizza you can eat.

SHORTBREAD WITH ROSEMARY
AND CANDIED GINGER

Through Delancey, Brandon and I got to know Christina Choi, chef-owner of Nettletown, an all-too-short-lived restaurant in the Eastlake neighborhood of Seattle. Christina had big eyes and a great laugh, a passion for wild foods and foraging, and her cooking was complex and inventive. If you were very, very lucky, you got to taste her crisp-seared wild salmon sandwich, with a swipe of peanut butter, pickled carrots and onions, and sprigs of dill, parsley, and fennel fronds. Christina died of complications from a brain aneurysm in December of 2011, at the age of thirty-four. We miss her, and Nettletown.

This recipe is my attempt to re-create one of the cookies she kept in a glass jar on the front counter of the restaurant. I was able to find her basic shortbread recipe online, on a blog she kept for a while, but I've had to wing it on the quantities of rosemary and ginger. I make my cookies a little smaller and thinner than hers, but all in all, I hope she would approve.

Christina made these cookies as slice-and-bakes, but the dough can also be rolled out and cut into any shapes you like.

1/2 cup (100 g) sugar

2 sticks (226 g) unsalted butter, at room temperature

2 cups (280 g) unbleached all-purpose flour

1/2 teaspoon fine sea salt

1 tablespoon (about 4 g) finely chopped fresh rosemary leaves

1/3 cup (60 g) chopped candied ginger

In the bowl of a stand mixer fitted with the paddle attachment, combine the sugar and butter. Beat until light and fluffy, scraping down the sides of the bowl as needed with a rubber spatula.

In a small bowl, whisk together the flour, salt, and rosemary. Add to the mixer bowl, and beat on low speed until the flour is absorbed and the dough begins to form large clumps that pull away from the sides of the bowl. Add the candied ginger, and mix briefly to incorporate. Divide the dough between two pieces of plastic wrap or parchment paper, and shape it into roughly 1 1/2-inch-diameter logs. Wrap, and refrigerate the dough logs for a few hours or overnight, until good and firm.

When you're ready to bake the cookies, preheat the oven to 300°F. Line two baking sheets with parchment paper.

Remove the logs from the refrigerator, and

while they're still very cold, slice them into 1/4-inch-thick rounds. Arrange the cookies 1 inch apart on the prepared baking sheets. Bake for 20 to 25 minutes, until the edges are pale golden, rotating and switching the pans midway through. Transfer the cookies to a wire rack to cool completely.

These cookies will keep in an airtight container at room temperature for a week, if not longer. They can also be frozen.

Yield: about 60 cookies

EPILOGUE

The days are different now from how they were before the restaurant, but not in the way that I thought they would be. I don't have a formal title at Delancey. I'm not a professional cook. I'm mostly there during the daytime, before opening, the hours that no one sees. I like that. My work consists of tasting new dishes; filing invoices, paying bills, and organizing; making sure the bathroom is tidy (when it comes to getting a wad of paper towel into a trash can, a lot of people would be more successful if they were blindfolded and spun around); helping to write the menu and editing it for typos (Brandon tends to capitalize all nouns; he's German at heart); sending website updates to Sam; doing payroll and front-of-house scheduling; and running a relay race with our bookkeeper, passing tax information back and forth. I do the jobs that I'm good at and enjoy doing, which are mostly the

jobs that Brandon is bad at and hates doing. Logical enough, though it took a while
to figure out. Then Brandon does the jobs
he's good at, like making pizza and leading
the staff — being "the motherfucker in
front," as Chris Bianco succinctly put it.
One of the most loving things that Brandon
has ever done for me is to choose not to
teach me how to work the pizza station, so
that even in case of emergency, I will have
no obligation to step in. Not everyone is cut
out for being the motherfucker in front. In
case of emergency, we close for the night.

When we negotiated the lease for Delancey back in late 2008, we added a clause
that gave us first dibs on the space next
door, should the umbrella shop ever move
out. We might want to expand, we figured,
or maybe add a bar, a sort of waiting area
for the restaurant. The umbrella shop
moved to Pike Place Market in late April of
2012, and we — this time with muscle from
our contractor friend Joe Burmeister — set
to work turning the pocket-sized space into
a bar. Like Delancey, it was designed by my
cousin Katie and her friend Pantea, with a
lot of annoying interruptions from Brandon
and me. It's called Essex, after one of the
streets that crosses Delancey in Manhattan.
The Delancey Street and Essex Street

subway stops share a station; our Delancey and our Essex share two bathrooms, a hallway, and a kitchen. Same thing, basically.

Initially, we thought of Essex as a place for people to hang out and have a drink before eating at Delancey, but as the opening date got closer, we began to think of it as something bigger: a small restaurant with an emphasis on cocktails, a place where Brandon and our cooks could play around with making and serving things that don't fit at Delancey. For a couple of years, Brandon has been tinkering with various herbs and flowers, teaching himself how to make bitters and liqueurs that we now serve at Essex. He's made liqueurs out of everything from wood oven–roasted radicchio to fennel, wild watercress, Pixie tangerine peels, and cilantro root. My favorite, called Burg's Extra-Special Orange, is his nod to Grand Marnier, made from three kinds of citrus and aged for four months in rye barrels. It's named for my dad, who would have loved it. Like the drinks, the food at Essex reflects Brandon's love for making things that other, more sane people would probably outsource. We make the cultured butter that we serve with bread, and the mustard we serve with house-made beer-boiled pretzels. The cooks are curing fish now, and over the course of each year, they pickle hundreds of quarts of vegetables and fruits to serve with cheeses and cured meats. Essex opened in mid-August of 2012, and I gave birth to our first child, a baby girl named June, on September ninth.

I see now that Delancey was the beginning of a process that will continue to shape, stretch, and reshape us. I don't know what we would be without it, that process, that constant growing, but it doesn't mean that I crave it the way Brandon does, or that I always like it. But I've learned now that we can withstand it, and that I can withstand it. I consider it a great personal victory that I could be eight months pregnant, helping to pick out crown molding for a bar that, for all I knew, could open on the same day that I went into labor, and not have to breathe into a paper bag. Of course, after Essex, Brandon also wants to open a distillery. He bought a briefcase-sized copper whiskey still a couple of years ago, though it's never left its box, so we'll see what becomes of the idea. Either way, when we were in the car together recently, driving to join one of our cooks for an Essex menu meeting, I filed an official request that we not open anything else — not the distillery, not anything — for five years.

"Oh, of course not," he said. "I'm done! I just want to enjoy what we have." He went quiet for a minute. "I mean, I definitely won't do anything for three years."

"Five years."

When I was a kid, my mother used to sometimes go on vacation by herself, to New York to shop and see a couple of shows, or to some fitness spa where, this being the '80s, her souvenir would be an oversized calf-length hoodie sweatshirt with something or other spelled out in bubble letters on the back. While Mom was gone, my dad and I would eat bachelor-style meals of hot dogs and baked beans, and in the mornings, he would endeavor to impose some order on my thick hair before we left to run carpool. It was normal to me that my parents did things separately sometimes — that my mother should go away by herself, or that, on another occasion, my father might go fishing with the guys. But I imagine that my mother in particular had to fight for it — not so much with my father, but with strangers or even friends, people who found it odd that a married woman, a mother, would leave her spouse and young child not for work or some other imposition, but for some time alone, for herself. My parents didn't have any kind of storybook marriage, but the older I get, the more I admire their belief in independence. It wasn't necessarily easy, but they had a certain kind of trust. They let each other be individual people even as they chose to be together.

Brandon was twenty-seven years old when we opened Delancey. I was thirty. I was married to him, but in a sense, I hardly knew him. I didn't know that he had a head for business, or that he could lead people, or that, after going through the multiyear rigmarole of opening a restaurant, he would even still be interested in it. And I didn't know that he would be right: that it *would,* in fact, realize everything that matters to us. I learned that only by letting him do it — "letting" in the very loosest interpretation, through clenched teeth and with a certain amount of screaming.

In return, I got to discover something in myself, albeit also with some screaming. I have never been good at change. Even small, positive changes, like Brandon getting a haircut, can upend me for a day or two. But I thought somehow that, by throwing myself into Delancey, I could trick my system, beat change at its own game. I couldn't. I couldn't change in the way that I had wanted to: I couldn't be a professional cook; a consistently game, supportive spouse; or even a pleasant person. But Delancey did change me. I saw my own limits, walked right up to the edge and even over it once or twice, and I saw that I could be all right again. I could be more than all right: I could be happy. I learned that my life could reshape itself completely, and that, maybe if I stopped trying to fight it or to hurriedly reshape myself before anything else did, I could instead let it slowly guide me, bend me, and bring me along. Brandon saw that before I did, I think; that's why he helped get me out of the kitchen at Delancey. He let me go so that I could let go.

We took a trip together, though it didn't always feel that way. We got to have a small victory in the end: a successful business. Of course, the story of that business is not finished. (It'll never really be finished; there's always a piece of equipment to fix or an employee to replace.) I don't know what's coming next, not really. I can't see much further than the bar and the baby. But I hope that we can always do this: that I can let him go, that he can let me go, and that, wherever it takes us, we find the way back.

ACKNOWLEDGMENTS

This book exists because I've had a lot of wonderful people on my side.

To Antonia Allegra, Elissa Altman, Jessica Fechtor, Dorie Greenspan, Dorothy Kalins, and Luisa Weiss: you helped me to believe in this story, and to believe that I could write it. Thank you.

To Bruce Schoenfeld: once, over dinner, you told me something that you knew I needed to hear. You reminded me that Brandon and I are a team, and that, if I may paraphrase, what's good for one of us is (usually) good for both of us. You wise, wise man.

To Olaiya Land: you sat next to me while I hashed out the earliest plans for this book, and later, as I worked on the recipes, you always answered the phone when I called to ask dumb cooking questions. Thank you for your good cheer and your great taste.

To Brandi Henderson: for the rice pudding and ricotta recipes, for your contagious enthusiasm for milkshakes and liberal politics, for the hiking and the biking and the ledger on the walk-in door. Long live the Pantry!

To Sam Schick: thank you, friend, for our Chocolati work dates, for the many conversations about writing and reading and Springsteen, for caring about our restaurant as though it were your own (and it might as well be), for your constant friendship.

To Ben Smith: for many home-cooked meals in Ballard; for two weeks of espresso, quiet days, companionship, and strong cocktails in Berea; for being the Luigi to our Brandono.

To Matthew Amster-Burton: for our Remedy Teas work dates, for being my first reader *and* second reader *and* a recipe tester, for making me laugh week after week after week. (And to Laurie and Iris: thank you for June-sitting!)

To Trish Todd: for getting behind this book so wholeheartedly, for bearing with me, and for your remarkable patience, understanding, and care. You helped me learn how to tell this story.

To Michael Bourret: for being my best advocate and my cheerleader. I owe you many, many pizzas.

330

To Katie Caradec and Pantea Tehrani: for designing the hell out of Delancey (and Essex), for not killing Brandon, for your smarts and your excellent taste.

To Kristen Bergsman (and Stanley the Dog): for keeping me company from down the hall.

To Kim Kent: for testing recipes, even with a bum knee! (And to Niah Bystrom: thank you for delivering groceries.)

To the readers of *Orangette:* thank you for reading, for caring, for cheering. I get to do what I do because of you.

To the Delancey regulars: for being there every night, and for being as crazy about pizza as we are.

To the old friends, new friends, and family members who helped us build Delancey: Ryan and Kristen Bergsman, Ryan Thompson, Mohini Patel Glanz, Myra Kohn, Tara Austen Weaver, Matthew and Laurie Amster-Burton, Shauna and Dan Ahern, Keaton and Mark Whitten, Jodell and Michael Egbert, Franz Gilbertson, Anne Catherine Kruger, Ralph and Wanda Nuxoll, Dave and Cubby Bartanen, Ashley and Gabe Rodriguez, Ben Smith, Bonnie Whiting, Sam Schick, Heidi Byrnes, Rebecca Leone, Jimmy Chorley, John Vatcher, Olaiya Land, John Streimikes, Katie Caradec,

Pantea Tehrani, Susan Kaplan, Renee Erickson, Carla Leonardi, Toni Wizenberg, David Wizenberg, Bill Pettit, and Kathy Platt. You scrubbed rusty refrigerator shelves, cleaned bathrooms, loaned trucks, fed us, gave us your weekends, taught us everything we know. You made this restaurant.

To the Delancey staff, past and present: you are the blood and bones of this restaurant. Because of you, we're a family.

To Bill Pettit and Kathy Platt: for your ardent support of Delancey (especially its chocolate chip cookies), for your errand-running and lunch-delivering during those crazy first days, for helping to make Brandon who he is.

To Tina Baylis: for that day at Johns Hopkins when you asked me to tell you about this book and said how much you wanted to read it. I miss you, Teens. I still can't believe it.

To Burg: there's so much of you in Delancey. I wish you could see it.

To Mom: for everything. Everything.

To June: you are the life, and the heart, of the pizza party. I know you will grow up seeing in us the many stresses of small business ownership, but I hope Delancey will also feed you, and nurture you, and feel like home.

And to Brandon: for your vision and your energy, for welcoming me in and helping me to get out, for doing the work with me every day, for your love, for you. Thank you.

RECIPE INDEX

ABOUT THE AUTHOR

Molly Wizenberg is the voice behind *Orangette,* named the best food blog in the world by the *London Times.* Her first book, *A Homemade Life: Stories and Recipes from My Kitchen Table,* was a *New York Times* bestseller, and her work has appeared in *Bon Appétit, The Art of Eating,* and *The Washington Post.* She also co-hosts the hit podcast *Spilled Milk.* She lives in Seattle with her husband, Brandon Pettit, their daughter, June, and two dogs named Jack and Alice. She and Brandon own and run the restaurants Delancey and Essex.

The employees of Thorndike Press hope you have enjoyed this Large Print book. All our Thorndike, Wheeler, and Kennebec Large Print titles are designed for easy reading, and all our books are made to last. Other Thorndike Press Large Print books are available at your library, through selected bookstores, or directly from us.

For information about titles, please call:
(800) 223-1244

or visit our Web site at:
http://gale.cengage.com/thorndike

To share your comments, please write:
Publisher
Thorndike Press
10 Water St., Suite 310
Waterville, ME 04901